Sexegesis

An Evangelical Response to
Five Uneasy Pieces on Homosexuality

Editors—Michael Bird and Gordon Preece

Published June 2012 by Anglican Press Australia
an imprint of Anglican Youthworks
PO Box A287, Sydney South NSW 1235
Australia

Contents

Acknowledgements

This entire project was instigated by one faithful Christian lady, who was so distraught by the prospect that an incorrect interpretation of God's Word would be without counter that she felt compelled to do something about it.

As Paul writes in 1 Corinthians 12, the body is made up of many members and each with different gifts. This work is a testimony to all those who agreed to put aside other projects and make this book a priority utilising the gifts that the Lord has blessed them with.

There has been a very large team involved, including the writers, editors, publishers, administers and financial backers; however, it would be amiss not to single out Anne Milton (the faithful Christian lady) for her work behind the scenes and Gordon Preece (main editor) who somehow managed to squeeze this project into his already impossibly busy schedule.

It is also appropriate at this time to acknowledge the three main organisations behind coordinating this project—The New Cranmer Lobby in Brisbane, Ethos: EA Centre for Christianity and Society in Melbourne and Youthworks in Sydney; each of which has committed personal time and resources to bringing this work into reality.

We would also like to thank Paul Barnett for writing his thoughtful piece at short notice, due to an unexpected change in content.

New Cranmer Lobby Brisbane

Contributors

Peter Adam is recently retired Principal of Ridley Melbourne and Vicar Emeritus of St. Jude's Carlton.

Paul Barnett, former Anglican Bishop of North Sydney, Australia, is an Honorary Associate in Ancient History at Macquarie University, Sydney and Teaching Fellow at Regent College, Vancouver and Moore College, Sydney.

Michael F. Bird is Lecturer in Theology and New Testament at Crossway College in Brisbane, Australia.

Denise Cooper-Clarke is a researcher with Ethos (Evangelical Alliance Centre for Christianity and Society), and an adjunct lecturer in Ethics at Ridley Melbourne.

Sarah Harris is Lecturer in New Testament at Carey College in Auckland, New Zealand.

Barry McGrath is an Anglican clergyman in inner-city Sydney with young adult children.

Gordon Preece is Director of Ethos, Priest-in Charge at Yarraville Anglican Parish, and visiting lecturer/consultant in Ethics at Macquarie Centre for Applied Finance, Ridley Melbourne, and Christian Super.

Katy Smith is Lecturer in Old Testament at Bible College of South Australia.

Lindsay Wilson is Senior Lecturer in Old Testament at Ridley Melbourne.

Preface

PETER ADAM

It is an honour to be invited to write the Preface for this book. I have read it with great interest, and I am delighted at the quality, depth and breadth of this presentation of Evangelical perspectives on the Bible's teaching on homosexuality. This book not only gives a suitable reply to *Five Uneasy Pieces,* but also makes a useful contribution to the current debate.

One response to this book may be that the authors demonstrate an obsession with human sexuality. But we did not begin this debate. The issue has been raised by others in the church, as also by current patterns in our Western society. We are responding to those who want to change widely-accepted biblical standards of Christianity of the last two thousand years. Of course they are free to recommend such changes, but if they do, they must expect others to reply to their challenges.

I suspect there are two fundamental issues in this general debate. Firstly a widespread belief in absolute personal autonomy leads us to resist any limitation on our actions. Secondly, popular psychological ideas lead us to think that resisting our deepest desires will harm us as people.

It is important to recognise that those who express the views outlined in this book do so not only because of a desire to teach what the Bible teaches, but also do so out of compassion. If it is true that homosexual practice is contrary to the best plan of God for our lives, and if it places us in danger of God's judgment, then it is an act of compassion to tell and warn people that this is the case. Compassion is the motivation for many warnings in our society. We warn people that smoking damages health, as we warn them not to drink and drive. Those who hold the views described in this book have a duty to love their neighbours, and warn them of what may damage them.

Those who do this task of warning will be accused of 'homophobia'. This attempts to muddy the waters by hinting at unhealthy psychological motivations. This psychologising trivialises public debate, and is a way of avoiding the substantial personal, moral, ethical, theological, and Biblical issues.

Furthermore, they may be accused of stirring up hatred. That is a very serious charge, and raises an issue of some complexity. May we not express opinions which others may use to justify violence? If we followed this as a general policy, it would close down a lot of human discussion, and reduce our capacity to engage in intellectual and public debate. This would then have serious political consequences, as we would be unable to debate serious issues, a dangerous situation for a democracy.

Australian Anglicans are committed to the Constitution of their church, which includes these words:

> This Church receives all the canonical scriptures of the Old and New Testaments as being the ultimate rule and standard of faith given by inspiration of God.[1]

I invite you to learn and listen to these Scriptures as you read this book.

---

1.   Constitution of the Anglican Church of Australia, Fundamental Declarations, 2.

Introduction

GORDON PREECE

Engaging Conversations

I write this introduction to *Sexegesis: An Evangelical Response to Five Uneasy Pieces on Homosexuality,* by Australasian Anglicans, as a response to the invitation to a conversation that Bishop Mark Burton mentions in his preface to *Five Uneasy Pieces* (*FUP* vii). I particularly write in response to the Introduction by the distinguished Michael Kirby. I was once thrilled as a young clergyman to sit opposite then Judge Kirby after a dinner address he gave at New College, University of NSW in the 1980s. I found him a most engaging conversation partner. I hope I can keep that conversation in mind in this more difficult conversation where, frankly, he adopts a more polemical tone, understandably in some ways, for there are high personal and ecclesiological stakes in this conversation, on both sides.

Sexegesis is literally exegesis or reading out from texts, texts on sex, specifically homosexuality. We've used the term deliberately because we believe that the *Five Uneasy Pieces* written by Australian Anglican scholars advocating a revisionist reading of the Bible on homosexuality, do not, apart from the Meg Warner and Alan Cadwallader pieces, spend much time on exegesis. They generally jump quickly to wider hermeneutical or interpretive issues regarding Scripture's relationship to other authorities, such as science or experience, or contemporary ethical and cultural standards. We don't ignore these, but want to first emphasis the text on sex, in its context, without risking the contemporary clamour around this issue drowning out the voice of God in the voice(s) of Scripture. As sociologist Peter Berger once said: "whereas Judas betrayed Jesus with a kiss, today we betray him with a hermeneut c."[2] Both sides of this debate need to beware of this.

I also write soon after conversations with the Global Atheist Convention held in Melbourne on April 13-15, 2012. In bringing it and his Introduction together, I am not implying that Justice Kirby is a non-believer, but observing a methodological similarity between the New Atheists and his privileging of new discoveries of science over against old dogma and the *art* of traditional interpretation. Kirby claims that the source for the churches' "terrible pickle over human sexuality" is "the age old problem of the text. And the human disinclination in the face of *new* knowledge, to adjust to the necessities of *new* thinking" (xix, my italics). This almost automatic rejection of the old or traditional is puzzling in contradiction with, for instance, Justice Kirby's support of the monarchy, or Anglican liturgy, or many traditional legal practices. This seems to deny what G.K. Chesterton calls "the democracy of the dead."[3]

My conversation with Michael Kirby reminds me of one I had with then Archbishop of Brisbane Peter Hollingworth soon after the 1998 Lambeth Bishops Conference of Anglican bishops which voted resoundingly, by 526 to 70, against the practice of homosexuality, and for a continued process of listening to Scripture and homosexuals. Hollingworth wrote to his diocese using similar language to Kirby, contrasting these new scientific understandings of the liberal and open West with the new and somewhat naïve and hermeneutically unsophisticated understanding of Scripture on homosexuality by African bishops. I asked Archbishop Hollingworth then, as I ask Justice Kirby now, why 'new' is positive when referring to the disputed findings of modern science concerning homosexuality and negative

2. Cited by Graham Cole, on 21/7/00 at Ridley College speaking on "The Ordination of Women & Practising Homosexuals."

3. See G.R. Preece, "The Democracy of the Dead: Homosexuality and Tradition," in Brian Edgar and Gordon Preece, *Whose Homosexuality? Which Authority? Homosexual Practice, Marriage, Ordination, and the Church* (Interface 9/1 and 2, May and October 2006, Adelaide: ATF) ch. 4. This responded to ch. 3 by Muriel Porter, "Homosexuality in Christian Tradition," which like Kirby, takes a Whig, progressive, evolutionary view of history.

concerning the traditional interpretation of Scripture adopted by the African Bishops at Lambeth, though they are relatively new to the faith.[4] I ask the same question of current Brisbane Archbishop and Primate of Australia, Phillip Aspinall, who says 'that we do know now more than the biblical authors knew about homosexuality. That must be taken into account as must the experience of homosexual people who are committed to Christ and the Church and who do not believe they are called to celibacy."[5] Perhaps we know more scientifically now,[6] and have more open homosexual experience to draw on, but that does not give either source the final word in a Christian conversation. Further, Archbishop Aspinall's March 2012 *Ad Clerum* to Brisbane clergy commended the study of *Five Uneasy Pieces* without citing other books taking a different position or even, like Edgar's and my *Whose Homosexuality?*, containing both sides. That is a monologue, not a dialogue.

Inconvenient Truths

Justice Kirby cites a few "Inconvenient Truths" or key examples of this new knowledge. First is Alfred Kinsey the mid 20th century pioneer of sexuality research showing that homosexuals and bisexuals were "widespread", not an evil and "tiny minority", "wickedly choosing" unnatural sexual expressions. While Kirby doesn't cite Kinsey's alleged conclusion of 10% of the population having a homosexual orientation, as he commonly has, now putting it at "say four percent" (xxiii), he still accepts Kinsey's authority. This despite the fact that new research has shown the 10% figure to be wrong by c. 300%.[7]

---

4.   *Focus* No. 240, October, 1998, 2 and my reply *Focus* No. 241, November, 1998, 2.

5.   "From the Archbishop", *Focus* August 2003, 2.

6.   See David Clarke, "Science and Sexuality," in *Beyond Stereotypes: Christians & Homosexuality* (Box Hill: EA, 2009), 29-35 and Robert A. J. Gagnon, *The Bible and Homosexual Practice: Texts and Hermeneutics* (Nashville: Abingdon, 2001), 380-432.

7.   See J. Harvey, et al, "Sex in Australia: The Australian study of health and relationships," *The Australian and New Zealand Journal of Public Health* 27/2, (2003), 230-33, the largest, most thorough survey. It found 97.4% of men

Kinsey's flawed and fraudulent report fuelled the sexual revolution.[8]

Kirby's second argument is that homosexual and bisexual inclinations were "the very expression of *their* nature ... some (perhaps many) cases ... were the product of genetic hard-wiring, over which the[y] ... had no more choice than they did over their skin and hair colour, ... gender and left or right handedness" (xix). I have heard something similar from a gay Uniting Church clergyman who from a young age felt himself attracted to the bare-chested Indians in cowboy movies.

Yet we should also hear the following from a range of disciplines, gender and political persuasions. Prominent UK gay rights activist Peter Tatchell has said:

> [A]n influence is not the same as a cause. Genes and hormones may

---

identified as heterosexual, 1.6% as gay and 0.9% bisexual. For women 97.7% identified as heterosexual, 0.8% as lesbian. Pagan bi-sexual and culture critic Camille Paglia says: "The 10 percent figure, servilely repeated by the media, was pure propaganda, and it made me, as a scholar, despise gay activists for their unscrupulous disregard for the truth." "Rebel Love: Homosexuality," in her *Vamps and Tramps* (New York: Vintage, 1994), 74.

8. See Judith A. Reisman and Edward W. Eichel, *Kinsey, Sex and Fraud: The Indoctrination of a People* eds. J Gordon Muir and John H. Court (Lafayette, La: Huntington House, 1990) and James H. Jones, *Alfred C. Kinsey* (New York: WW Norton, 1998). Cf. E. Michael Jones, *Degenerate Moderns: Modernity as Rationalized Sexual Misbehaviour* (San Francisco: Ignatius, 1993) seeing various sexperts' rationalisations o their own behaviour reflecting what Paul says in Romans 1:32: "they know God's decree that those who practise such things [from a conventional vice list plus homosexual practice] deserve to die—yet they not only do them but even applaud others who practise them." Psychologist Ronald Conway says "three serious objections against his [Kinsey's] work have persisted across the ideological spectrum. First, his interview samples were too skewed toward the central and north-eastern American states, and too biased towards college folk, prison inmates and deviate groups. Second, his frame of reference was too crassly literal and biological and lacked psychological nuance. Third, his treatment of raw data from disparate sources was statistically flawed." However, Kinsey is more cautious than gay lobby groups using the figure of 10% of men being gay. This referred to exclusive male to male sex for a three year period between 16 and 65. "His own actual figure for predominantly homosexual men in his sample was only four per cent." "Fifty Years After the Kinsey Report," *Quadrant* September 1998, 67.

predispose a person to one sexuality rather than another. But that's all. Predisposition and determination are two different things.

There is a major problem with gay gene theory, and with all theories that posit the biological programming of sexual orientation. If heterosexuality and homosexuality are, indeed, genetically predetermined (and therefore mutually exclusive and unchangeable), how do we explain bisexuality or people who, suddenly in mid-life, switch from heterosexuality to homosexuality (or vice versa)? We can't.[9]

Frank Furedi, Professor of Sociology at University of Kent adds:

> Thankfully, the experience of human endeavour tells us that who we are need not be determined by a biological accident. Yes, our genes influence our behaviour. But this does not determine who we are. We are not the slaves of our biology and possess a formidable capacity to make our own world and on a good day to even choose who we want to be."

John D'Emilio, US gay activist and professor of history of women's and gender studies at the University of Illinois, Chicago, says this on the convenient 'truth' of the 'born gay' theory of Kirby and others:

> "[B]orn gay" is an idea with a large constituency, LGBT [Lesbian, Gay, Bisexual, Transexual] and otherwise. It's an idea designed to allay the ingrained fears of a homophobic society and the internalised fears of gays, lesbians, and bisexuals. What's most amazing to me about the "born gay" phenomenon is that the scientific evidence for it is thin as a reed, yet it doesn't matter. It's an idea with such social utility that one doesn't need much evidence in order to make it attractive and credible."[10]

---

9.   On the scientific evidence see N. E. Whitehead, *My Genes Made Me Do It: a Scientific Look At Sexual Orientation* rev. 2nd edition, 2010, www.mygenes. co.nz. On choice see the Dutch homosexual with doctorates in biology and theology, Pim Pronk, *Against Nature? Types of Augmentation Against Homosexuality* (Grand Rapids: Eerdmans, 1993). He argues that no one is "born" homosexual; there is always choice.

10.   This collection of quotes comes from the Australian Christian Lobby (ACL) Media Release 14/2/12.

Talk about gay genes has proven premature.[11] After the initial euphoria at the completion of the Human Genome Project there was a tendency towards genetic determinism. The balance is swinging back to a consensus that environment and genetics/neurology, culture and nature, are mutually interactive. Francis Collins, head of the human genome project states that homosexuality is "a predisposition, not a pre-determination."[12] That predisposition can be a very powerful one, but it does not resolve those with it from human responsibility for what they do with it. That is both a burden and a hope.

As Stanton L. Jones aptly sums up:

> We know much more now than we did 10 and 30 years ago about the emotional well-being of homosexual persons, the complicated interaction of nature and nurture in the causation of sexual orientation, of the complicated, limited, and difficult possibilities of sexual orientation malleability, of the functional and descriptive characteristics manifest in same-sex partnerships and of the contours of the psychological identities of homosexual persons. The contributions of science to this complicated area, however, remain sketchy, limited and puzzling. It is remarkable how little scientific humility is in evidence given the primitive nature of our knowledge.

> Perhaps if our culture can recognise the fluid and incomplete nature of our knowledge of the homosexual condition, if we can recognise the limits of reason, we may be able to create a public space where differing parties agree to disagree and give each other room to live in civility. But the best ecclesiastical, professional, legal and social policy will not be founded on falsehoods or on grotesque and indefensible simplifications, but on a clearheaded grasp of reality in

---

11.   Paglia speaks strongly of how gay activist "fbs and fabrications continue, now about the still-fragmentary evidence for a genetic link to homosexuality. I am ... unpersuaded, thus far, by multigenerational and twin studies that claim to have found evidence for a genetic basis for homosexuality..." *Vamps and Tramps* 74.

12.   http://b1163w.blu163.mail.live.com/mail/. For a balanced view of scientific evidence on homosexuality see David Clarke, "Scientific Reason and Homosexuality," Ch. 6 in Edgar and Preece, *Whose Homosexuality?*

all its complexities, as well as on a humble recognition of all that we do not know.[13]

Kirby accuses the conservative Anglican, Catholic, Orthodox and Pentecostal churches of prevaricating in the face of the inevitable, undeniable scientific evidence, clinging "onto *old* beliefs" and citing "*old* Biblical texts in support of doing so" (xx, my italics). But from well informed scientific perspectives, not pink propaganda, it sounds like those churches are being appropriately humble. Justice Kirby seems to be prematurely pronouncing the verdict while the jury is still out, a victim of scientific hubris or fundamentalism, adopting what C.S. Lewis calls "chronological snobbery."[14] By contrast, the ex-Catholic Paglia wants the Church to be clearly Christian: "The institutional religions, Catholic and Protestant, carry with them the majesty of history. Their theology is impressive and coherent. Attempts to revise or dilute that theology for present convenience seem to me misguided."[15]

It is also important to note Kirby's misconceived analogy between disagreement with homosexual practice and racism or sexism: "Like the black majority of South Africa they [gays] must forever be cast into a kind of sexual apartheid" (xxiii). His championing of Bishop Desmond Tutu's linking of his opposition to apartheid and opposition to *hatred* of gay Christians obviously holds, but not opposition to all discrimination, as many extend civil rights discourse to.[16] All people

---

13.   Stanton L. Jones, "Same-sex Science," *First Things* (February 2012), 27-33.

14.   *Surprised by Joy* (San Diego: Harcourt Brace Jovanovich, 1955), 206. See further my "The Democracy of the Dead" in *Whose Homosexuality?*

15.   "The Joy of Presbyterian Sex," *The New Republic* (2 December 1991), 24-27.

16.   My Evangelical Episcopal priest friend Will Messenger from the Diocese of Massuchusetts says most supporters of homosexual practice, ordination and marriage, like Tutu and Kirby, see a straight line from Martin Luther King to these practices. However, racial discrimination is against persons, not actions, as is the kind of biblical "discrimination" this book supports. The positive connotation can still be heard in the old Benson and Hedges ad—"for the discriminating smoker." Here I am arguing for the church's right to govern its own life, to make discriminating, discerning decisions, by its own scriptural standards. This is

are called to be discriminating in a positive sense of being discerning. Christians discern what behaviours are appropriate primarily on the basis of the biblical portrayal of male-female relations in Scripture. In fact I make a strong case in Chapter 1, that the basic problem with homosexual practice is its sexism, discriminating against the opposite, equal and complementary sex (Gen 1:26-28; Rom 1:20ff).

An Anglican Compromise

Kirby next argues for not only a middle way of adaptation of liturgical forms on things "in their own nature indifferent," as in the Preface to the 1662 Book of Common Prayer but "in the understanding of sacred texts" (xx-xxi). Here he makes a category mistake between things seen scripturally as spiritually or morally indifferent (cf. Romans 14:13-23 on foods and days of worship), and therefore adaptable in worship services, and Scripture's moral teaching itself, as if the Prayer Book is its equal.

The architect of Prayer Book Anglicanism, Thomas Cranmer, after whom our sponsor the Brisbane New Cranmer Lobby is named, saw no such equivalence. Scripture is regarded by Cranmer, in his "True and Catholick Doctrine of the Sacraments," as the authoritative norm, above the relative norms of tradition and reason (later, experience was separated out by John Wesley).[17] Classical Anglicans have a ladder, not an equal table of authorities. Although the other authorities influence our reading of Scripture, in what Grant Osborne calls *The Hermeneutical Spiral*,[18] they do not supplant it or suppress its voice. In practice for Kirby and the other *FUP* authors the equal table has some longer legs, like science and the experience of practising homosexuals, that give the table a decidedly unstable bearing.

---

different to what standards the State should use in a pluralistic, democratic society. However, this is not the same as re-defining marriage.

17.   See Graham Cole, "Sola Scriptura: Some Historical and Contemporary Perspectives," *The Churchman* 104, (1990), 20-34.

18.   Revised and expanded 2nd edition, Downers Grove, IVP, 2006.

Michael Kirby, and fellow author Peta Sherlock, who sees most sexual ethics as matters of indifference, without scriptural guidance,[19] make a category mistake in accommodating scriptural authority on matters of morality to legitimate variation in liturgy on matters of indifference. In this they confuse what's right with rites.

Kirby's downgrading of the authority of Scripture to that of liturgy is matched by his elevation of the disputed 'discoveries that science is presenting' as almost papally infallible or irrefutable. This premature solidifying of scientific authority as the basis of Christian and sexual identity is matched by the gay lobby's tendency to prematurely set in stone, as a matter of concrete identity, the 'liquid' or ambiguous sexuality[20] of vulnerable people, particularly adolescents. While there are genuine pastoral motives involved, such as saving young gays from suicide, the cure may be worse than the illness, making unstable gay sexuality in postmodernity, into the still point of personal and political identity.

Then Justice Kirby turns personal in response to a sense of personal attack on gays. Churches could continue, he charges, to ignore scientific authority and "instruction" (cf 2 Tim 3:16) by rationalising their suppression of scientific truth by seeing GLBTIQ (Gay, Lesbian, Bisexual, Transsexual, Intersexual and Queer) people (including fellow believers) as "simply 'wicked'" or "wicked in themselves." But science makes this more difficult to argue, akin to people once preaching the "inherent wickedness" of women and left-handers (xxii).

Kirby's comments here are not characteristic of the great majority of Christians, conscious of their own sin, and not seeing homosexuals as any more "wicked in themselves" than they are—"all have sinned and fall short of the glory of God" (Rom 3:23). He sadly seems unable to distinguish between person and action. I understand that in a sexually saturated society that idolatrously and rhetorically makes

---

19.   "Reading Romans as Anglicans: Romans 1:26-27," *Five Uneasy Pieces 43.*

20.   See Zygmunt Bauman, *Liquid Love: On the Frailty of Human Bonds* (Cambridge UK: Polity, 2003), 54-55.

sexuality the basis of selfhood, that rejection of homosexual practice (not orientation) will often feel like rejection of the person, however hard one tries to avoid it. But to deny this everyday distinction we use on all sorts of other issues, is to give into a form of ethical emotivism and subjectivism. In Kirby's view, to refuse to discriminate against people of homosexual orientation, but then deny them sexual expression, is to patronise and oppress homosexuals. It is to deny them expression of "what follows *naturally* (my italics) for them because of their sexual orientation or gender identity." But this is to load the dice toward a subjective or solipsistic definition of the natural, for 'me', rather than one based on God's creation, for humanity, and its flourishing (Rom 1:24-25).

Let me stress again that I do not underestimate the enormity of homosexually oriented people living a celibate lifestyle, anymore than I do for the millions of single Christians, especially women (given they often outnumber Christian males by c. 60 to40%), living chastely. Kirby says passionately that people, like the writers of this book, say to homosexually oriented people that: "They must never have lovers with whom they can share acts of physical intimacy. They must never create domestic arrangements of tenderness and love. ... And no faithful, long-term relationships between them must be recognised. No desire for children must be fulfilled... No civil law should be changed to recognise the truth and reality of this minority... This is the command of Scripture. It must be obeyed" (xxii).

Sadly, Kirby has abandoned his judge's robes for the wig of prosecutorial rhetoric, no doubt deserved for the years when gay relationships were unrecognised. But his caricature is unrecognisable to probably the majority of Australian Christians today, who take a conservative, but compassionate approach to sexual social change. These, like me, recognise the difference between sin and crime in modern liberal democratic societies. They largely supported the dropping of the raft of discriminatory legislation against GLBTIQ people.[21]

---

21. For example my two Centre for Applied Christian Ethics (CACE) Newsletters 'Updated Response to Anti-Discrimination Board on Homosexual Adoption

Further, the church has for centuries offered forms of wholesome relational and physical intimacy—"greet one another with a holy kiss", says Paul (1 Cor 16:20). Note too the wonderful film of intimate monastic life in Algeria, "Of Gods and Men", following "Into the Silence", and numerous TV explorations of monastic life. Should the church reconsider these practices in a contemporary, culturally adapted form?[22]

An Unstable Resolution

Instead, Kirby believes "an unstable resolution" of respecting homosexual orientation but rejecting homosexual behaviour is falling apart, since "a desire for sexual expression is part of the powerful hard-wiring of every human being. Celibacy does not come naturally to humans," nor at all to other species. Further, celibate communities have been so "disappointing" and "damaging" because of its unreasonable demands" (xxiii). Kirby's description of the parlous state of contemporary celibate communities, declining in numbers and regarded by many as a synonym for paedophilia, is a common one in our culture. But his prescription, baptising what is as what ought to be, is not only a form of the famous naturalistic fallacy, a logical jump from an indicative or "is" statement to an imperative or "ought" statement, but a defeatist capitulation to the idolatry of sexual self-expression in western societies. The key word that Kirby uses unawares, is "part". Our sexual hard-wiring is not the whole of who we are, as Richard Hays' late gay friend Gary realised, against the idolatrous grounding of identity in our sexuality[23]—this applies to both hetero and homo-sexuality, to homo-phobia, and

---

& Marriage', Vol. 2, No.3, 1997 and 'Same-sex Relationships and the Law', Vol 3, No. 1, 1998, publically advocated reforming all discriminatory legislation against same-sex relationships not involving marriage (by definition heterosexual) or adoption (involving minors and thus not a standard liberal adult individual rights issue).

22. Inklings of this are found in the New Monastic Movement. See my "New Monasticism," *Arena Magazine* 08-09, (2009), 37-40.

23. Cited in Richard B. Hays, "Awaiting the Redemption of our Bodies," *Sojourners* (July 1991), 17.

homo-philia. Our identity, for gay and straight Christians, is first and foremost, in Christ.

I once counselled a young Christian man from Sydney's western suburbs who went straight from a heterosexual relationship with a friend of mine to going to the gay Metropolitan Community Church where he was paired up immediately at a house party. I encouraged him to see that his emerging homosexuality was not the whole of who he was, not his identity, but he was sucked into the vortex of gay identity sub-culture and politics.

As Hays, author of the best short biblical account of homosexual practice says:

> Despite the smooth illusions perpetrated by mass culture in the United States, sexual gratification is not a sacred right, and celibacy is not a fate worse than death. The Catholic tradition has something to teach ... Protestant communities. While mandatory priestly celibacy is unbiblical, a life of sexual abstinence can promote "good order and unhindered devotion to the Lord" (1 Cor 7:35). Surely it is a matter of some interest for Christian ethics that both Jesus and Paul lived without sexual relationships. It is also worth noting that 1 Corinthians 7:8-9, 25-40, commends celibacy as an option for everyone, not just for a special caste of ordained leaders. Within the church we should work diligently to recover the dignity and value of the single life.[24]

Contrast Hays' measured statement with Kirby's unmeasured "Celibacy does not come naturally to human beings ..." Kirby cites another discredited psychiatric authority, Freud, who declares Jesus, Paul and Mother Theresa, among others, as "unnatural?" (xxiii).

Many have advocated and approved changes to civil law for the recognition of gay relationships. But many, Christian, including me, and non-Christian, do not believe that the millennia long definition of marriage between a man a woman should be changed. The

---

24.   Richard B. Hays, *The Moral Vision of the New Testament: Community, Cross, New Creation; A Contemporary Introduction to New Testament Ethics* (HarperSanFrancisco, 1996), 401.

issue is not one of equality, for unequal legislation has been largely abandoned, but one of symbolic identity. And unfortunately there is legitimate concern among many Christians, that the huge hunger for symbolic social acceptance of gay marriage will not stop with the ceremony, but will demand being able to have it in church, be administered by any clergyperson, not spoken against from the pulpit etc. On liberal democratic and human rights grounds, Christians who are conservative on the homosexuality issue want their freedom of religion, not mere private religious rites and beliefs, but a literally 'binding' and public religious way of life, to be taught to their children and in their schools, and modelled by their ministers and employees. This should not be too much to ask in a democratic pluralist society which supposedly values the human right to free speech, parental rights to educate their children, and the corporate rights of groups, from footy clubs to employers, to have membership and behavioural codes.[25]

Justice Kirby sees two alternative "responses to the instability" of the unworkable church consensus of respecting homosexual orientation but rejecting its sexual expression. 1. Is to see it leading to a rapidly rising number of Australians, like his long-term partner, rejecting religion, through agnosticism, atheism or apathy. This follows his standard story of how religions, across the terrain of various moral issues, wage an increasingly vain rearguard action against scientifically proven contraception, IVF, women's sexuality etc. (xxiii). While I've argued that he has swallowed whole the myth of the warfare of science and religion and practises a form of irrational, utopian scientism (science as religion), Kirby's hunch about religion losing supporters over the homosexuality issue is supported by recent research, even by Christians like Mark McCrindle, providing a block to belief for c. 70% of respondents.[26]

---

25. Sadly this is not guaranteed under the Australian constitution unlike its U.S. cousin. This is one reason why conservative Christians are, in my view, mistaken in opposing human rights and responsibilities charters which would guarantee freedom of opinion. See www. isaiahone.org.au for more.

26. See Mark Brolly, "Church Abuse Biggest Obstacle to Belief: Survey," *TMA* 11/12/2011. The Australian Communities Report found 76% of c. 1000 people

This is clearly a problem for the churches, unless we accept Kirby's assumption we should therefore go with the flow, rather than swim against an irresistible tide. This seems to me to be not an *uneasy* way, but way too easy, avoiding the cost of discipleship. Kirby, like Schleiermacher's theological liberalism, is seeking to please 'religion's cultured despisers'.

Kirby's other alternative, or straw man, is 2. "business as usual." Here he again caricatures the Bible, dismissing Genesis and Leviticus as "old ways." This reminds me of my time as Residential Dean at Ridley College when having reminded some non-Christian residential university students of the college rule of no sex on campus, I was told that was so Medieval, though they seemed to think it was Medi-*evil*. I told the Principal Graham Cole who said "No, its much older than that." This parochialism of the present ignores the question of whether long standing biblical traditions are simply true to the maker's instructions for human flourishing and to the character of our complementary sexual ecology (see my Chapter 1). Kirby's pejorative linking of these to beliefs like the sun orbiting the earth, six day creationism, an anthropocentric, animal antagonistic view (xxiv) is simply untrue to what the majority of well-taught Christians have believed for millennia.

Justice Kirby's view is that "once the scientific truth about sexuality arrived in the human consciousness, like the earlier Darwinian evolution, it could not be suppressed." "There's nothing so powerful as an idea whose time has come" (xxiv). Again, Kirby confuses time and truth categories, as if calendars calculate truth. Time and truth are not the same. Kirby also exaggerates Darwin's influence on the rise of unbelief, as Charles Taylor's magisterial *A Secular Age* shows.[27] Similarly, by analogy to Darwin, he exaggerates the effect of so-called scientific discoveries about sexuality. Certainly, they

---

said church abuse was the top obstacle, but doctrines and practices about homosexuality were a "block" to belief for 59% of respondents.

27. Cambridge MA: Belknap, 2007, where Taylor says "I don't see the cogency of the supposed arguments from, say, the findings of Darwin to the alleged refutations of religion" (4).

have had important effects, but not nearly as much as contraceptive technologies like the pill, in moving the West away from a more reproductive to a more recreational sexual ethic.

Kirby then questions why God would make many people inclined to evil homosexual acts? His argument is little more than Lady Gaga's song *Born This Way*.[28] We won't therefore detail but simply state our earlier argument derived from Romans and argued in Ch. 1 and Ch. 4 of this book, that Paul's reference to unnatural sex is not to the reversal of an individual's sexual orientation, e.g. natural heterosexuals engaging in unnatural homosexual acts, but rather to something against the created order, our complementary sexual ecology as male and female.

Kirby again overreaches himself, asking "Why, in the face of evidence of their long-term loving and faithful relationships ..., would the almighty want to deny happy and loving contact, which, objectively does no harm to anyone? And actually strengthens society and is good for the physical and psychic health of all those concerned?" (xxv). Firstly, despite positive examples of long-term relationships like Justice Kirby and his same-sex partner, and Bob Brown and his, and Penny Wong and hers, these are rare, especially among men. Here Michael Kirby should consult the science that he so exalts.[29]

Further, the assertion of homosexual relationships enhancing physical health is simply denial of the scientific and medical evidence. Gay health activist Gabriell Rotello's book *Sexual Ecology*

---

28. From her album of that name, with narcissistic pop psychology lyrics such as: "Rejoice and love yourself today/'Cause baby, you were born this way/ No matter gay, straight or bi/Lesbian, transgendered life/I'm on the right track baby."

29. As Kevin Giles notes in a personal communication, "long-term exclusive male unions are the exception rather than the rule". A 1997 study of 2,583 homosexually active men in Australia found that only 28.5% had just one male partner that year. "Only 2.7% of those over 49 and 2.9% of those under 49 said they had had only one partner in their lifetime." Homosexuals usually do not deny these findings but reject monogamy. The 1995 *Advocate* survey of 2,500 lesbian readers showed an average ten sex partners in a lifetime. One study found that only 8% of homosexual men and 7% of homosexual women had had a relationship that lasted more than 4 years.

challenges various myths which are killing gays especially "the pervasive myth that humans have somehow transcended the limits of the biological world." Rotello argues that "the highly selective spread of HIV around the world shows that AIDS is ... an ecological epidemic that exploits certain behaviours, chief[ly] ... having large numbers of partners, straight or gay [and] the single riskiest sexual practice of all: anal sex."[30] And the psychological evidence is no more heartening.[31] For those who take a conservative perspective, this should not cause moralistic gloating, but great grief and compassion.

Hermeneutics and the Law, Art vs Science

Justice Kirby, while noting the Oxford English Dictionary definition of hermeneutics as "the art or science of interpretation, especially Scripture", returns quickly to stressing that legal and scriptural interpretation is a value-laden "art, not a science." The first part is legitimate, but not the second. For instance textual criticism about which texts are most original, is highly scientific in its rigorous methodology. But there is an art to it as well, as also in much science. All interpretation, in all disciplines, is value laden, but that does not mean that anything goes. We must bring our presuppositions to the table to be debated, not hide them in pseudo-scientific presumptions of objectivity. Michael Kirby is right to remind us of the way in which Scripture has been used to "provide the textual foundations for the worldwide animosity and even hatred towards sexual minorities" (xxv). But abuse does not deny use. We should repent of that abuse, particularly in the past, but also in the present,

---

30. Gabriell Rotello, *Sexual Ecology: AIDS and the Destiny of Gay Men*, (London: Plume, 1998), 188.

31. Thomas Schmidt, *Straight and Narrow?: Compassion and Clarity in the Homosexuality Debate* (Downers Grove, IVP: 1995) concludes: "For the vast majority of homosexual men and for a significant number of homosexual women—"even excluding AIDS"—sexual behaviour is obsessive, psychopathological and destructive to the body" including extraordinary drug and alcohol abuse. Cf. Jeffrey Satinover, *Homosexuality and the Politics of Truth* (Grand Rapids: Baker, 1996) on the political, not scientific process of the American Psychiatric Association normalising homosexuality.

as in the appalling Westboro Baptist with their "God Hates Gays" placards. They need to hear that those who refuse to turn from hostility to hospitality towards homosexuals are committing one of the sins of Sodom, inhospitality, and are therefore themselves sodomites. But we can still disagree with homosexual behaviour, without rejecting homosexual people.

So, conservatives on the homosexuality question have an onus on them to be more gracious and hospitable to homosexual people. But our more liberal brothers and sisters authoring "Five Uneasy Pieces, which Kirby regards as "full of ease and grace," need to hear Bonhoeffer's prophetic warnings against "cheap grace."[32] Kirby's concluding exhortation to "kindness and inclusiveness," depends on what *kind* of creatures we are, undifferentiated images of God, or differentiated, complementary as male and female, called to love each other in all their difference. It also depends on what kind of community the church is called to be, a bland form of contemporary, minimalistic, tolerant inclusivity,[33] or a catholic community,[34] living out an hospitable, generous Orthodoxy and orthopraxy, welcoming to what Christians have commonly believed in all times and places, and willing to be different to what a particular parochial part of the world believes in a particular time and place.

---

32. *The Cost of Discipleship* (London: SCM, 1958), Ch. 1.

33. As my doctoral mentor Miroslav Volf puts it powerfully: "Jesus was no prophet of 'inclusion' ... for whom the chief virtue was acceptance and the cardinal vice intolerance. [He] did scandalously include many who were normally excluded, but he also made the 'intolerant' demand of repentance and the 'condescending' offer of forgiveness." *Exclusion and Embrace* (Nashville: Abingdon, 1996), 72-73.

34. See Bryden Black, "Whose Language? Which Grammar?: 'Inclusivity' and 'Diversity' versus the Crafted Christian Concepts of Catholicity and Created Differentiation," in Edgar and Preece, *Whose Homosexuality? Which Authority?* Ch. 10.

CHAPTER 1

(Homo)Sex and the City of God: Sexual Ecology Between Creation and New Creation

GORDON PREECE

Introduction

This chapter[35] addresses what is the primary weakness of *Five Uneasy Pieces* (*FUP*), its complete lack of a creation theology. *FUP* addresses allegedly contested texts while ignoring the vast canvas of creation theology upon which they are written, giving the false impression of more biblical diversity than unity. We will firstly examine the homosexuality issue through a narrative theology of sexuality in a creation, fall and redemption narrative framework that illuminates the mystery of sexuality. We will look at our created sexual ecology, our fallen condition of sexual idolatry and ideology and the redemptive possibilities of sexual therapy anticipating the new creation and City of God, whose Tree of Life's evergreen and leaves "are for the healing of the nations" (Rev 22:2).

The biblical narrative of creation, fall and redemption both affirms and critiques our sexuality and points us to true north in the city of God, the new creation. That city contrasts both with the largely old middle class Christian and other family values advocates of the suburbs, or "burbos", and the sexually expressive "bobos" or bourgeois bohemians[36] of our growing and increasingly influential inner-cities. The split between these two groups, illustrated from the bobo side most notably in the influential TV series and double movie *Sex and the City,* set in the most postmodern of cities, New York, is sociologically where many of our contemporary social, ethical and church conflicts brew. Healing that split, by joining the personal and political, the body physical and body politic, through the biblical and Augustinian narrative of the City of God, is the task we now turn to.

---

35.   This is a reduced and adapted version of my "(Homo)Sex and the City of God," Ch. 12 in Brian Edgar and Gordon R. Preece, *Whose Homosexuality? Which Authority? Interface* Vol 9 Nos 1&2 (May and October 2006) used by kind permission of ATF Press, Adelaide.

36.   David Brooks, *Bobos in Paradise: The New Upper Class and How They Got There* (New York: Simon and Schuster, 2000).

1. Created Order—Sexual Ecology

The created order provides, in postmodern-speak, the pattern of our sexual *ecology*. We are gradually rediscovering our natural ecology, that everything is connected and has ecological consequences, from the butterfly flapping its wings in Cairns to the hurricane in Florida. It is ironic, then, that even the most left and green assume that somehow our humanity and sexuality stands outside this natural order in a subjective, ever-expanding erogenous zone of pure consumer choice.

By sexual ecology I mean that creation is in *kinds* or species (Gen 1) not just in our *minds*.[37] This contrasts strongly with the tragic recent Australian case of "Kevin," a female to male transsexual, lacking male genitalia, whose marriage to "Jennifer" has been recognised by The Family Court because "Kevin" has been living as a male for several years and *perceives* himself and *is perceived by society* as male.[38] This ruling capitulates to a Gnostic and "Alice in Wonderland"- like social constructionist view of sexuality. A word like "man" in the marriage act can now mean "just what I choose it to mean," according to Humpty Dumpty. Thus our own personally or socially produced biography trumps biology. As masters of the universe, we make up our own personal master-narratives. Oliver O'Donovan supports an English judge's verdict against the validity of an alleged marriage in a similar case, saying this leaves our gender floating above our biological sex like oil on water.[39] The Australian Government contested, but lost, the case on the grounds that "marriage" in The Marriage Act means people of the opposite

---

37. Following Oliver O'Donovan "The Natural Ethic," in D. F. Wright ed., *Essays in Evangelical Social Ethics* (Exeter: Paternoster Press, 1979), 19-25. These "kinds" are stable but open to evolutionary development.

38. Shown on ABC TV's *Australian Story* 31/3/03 as background to their transsexual lawyer's story. My use of this case is not meant to add to the tragic plight of transsexuals. I have often preached on "the good transsexual lawyer," who won a court-case for my family at a time of great need.

39. *Transsexualism* (Bramcote: Grove, 1982), 6. Judge Ormrod presided in Corbett v. Corbett, 1970.

biological sex (including, normally, reproductive potential), not just social gender. The ruling opened the way for homosexual marriage. The then Liberal government promptly closed the loophole, with the agreement of the Labor Opposition, by making the implicit and assumed opposite sex nature of "marriage" in the Marriage Act explicit. This loophole is likely to be opened again in the near future, though probably subject to High Court appeal.

Gordon Watson rightly takes the Australian Uniting Church Assembly's Sexuality Task Group to task for making the same subjective, solipsistic, and social constructionist mistake as the Family Court. They urge "that we must understand relationships in the Christian *koinonia* in terms of each individual's self-understanding" i.e. "perceived sexual orientation." The Church is to adopt the homosexual person's sexual self-understanding as an expression of compassion or unconditional acceptance. But this is compassion without a moral or cognitive compass. "God's 'compassion,' at great cost, recreates the creature as a creature." Based on Genesis 1:26-28's depiction of the image of God reflected or represented in our biological male and femaleness, Watson states that the argument "for legitimating homosexuality as a complementary Christian lifestyle in fact breaks the co-humanity of the human species as male and female and creates another species called homosexual."[40]

This created order or 'structured being (ordered ontology)"[41] includes the basic *difference* or *otherness* (also postmodern terms),

---

40. Gordon Watson, "The 'Çompassion' of God as a Basis for Christian Ethical Claims," in Murray A. Rae and Graham Redding ed. *More than a Single Issue* (Hindmarsh: Australian Theological Forum, 2000), 245-46, 250. Watson adds "The homosexual relationship cannot in principle be an image of such a compassionate relationship as is established by God in Christ's relationship with the Church [compared to marriage, for instance (Gen 2, Eph 5:21ff)], since it presupposes a relationship of like to like (i.e., homo). The relationship of Christ to the Church, however, is not one of like to like (250-51).

41. Ray S. Anderson, "Homosexuality and the Ministry of the Church: Theological and Pastoral Considerations," in *More than a Single Issue* 61.

or more conventionally, *complementarity* of male and female.[42] This is designed so that we image or represent God to each other relationally and sexually, and to creation through responsible rule (Gen 1:26-28). development and preservation (Gen 2:15). Homosexual practice is therefore wrong because it is a sexist (yet another postmodernism) rejection of that basic difference, and an overturning of the created order, exchanging natural relations for unnatural ones (Rom 1:26-27ff.).

Some argue against this that God's image refers to our intellectual, moral and spiritual similarity to God expressed in undifferentiated loving relationships. Therefore if homosexual relationships are loving and monogamous they are to be approved and recognised by marriage. However Ray Anderson, building on Karl Barth, critiques Emil Brunner's advocacy of this more vague view of God's image as expressed in I-thou relationships. Anderson and Barth show that God's image is spelt out specifically in terms of male–female biological and sexual differentiation. Diagram 1 below reflects Brunner's now common contemporary view of the moral and spiritual image not overlapping with biological sexual difference. Contrast Anderson's depiction of Barth's view of this overlap in Diagram 2 which also better reflects the diversity of the three persons within the unity of the Trinity. In Genesis 2:23, Eve's creation was more than a cloning of Adam. As Anderson summarises Barth, "the solitariness of Adam would not have been overcome by another male for such a one could not confront him as "another" but he would only recognise himself in it ... Consequently, Barth described homosexual practice as "humanity without the fellow man."[43]

---

42. By this I mean nothing of the loaded nature of "complementarian" when used against "egalitarian" in women's ordination debates. For the record, I am an egalitarian complementarian, and know ro biblical egalitarians who deny basic biological complementarity. *Vive la différence.*

43. Anderson, "Homosexuality" 58-62 citing Karl Barth, *Church Dogmatics III/4* (Edinburgh: T&T Clark, 1961), 166.

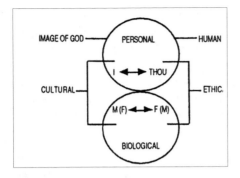

Diagram 1—Emil Brunner

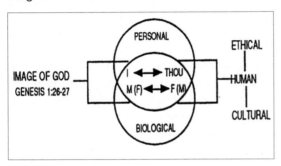

Diagram 2—Ray S. Anderson

Further, creation comes not only in differentiated kinds in a static or non-evolving way but also with God-given *ends* or purposes built in.[44] These include particular purposes; e.g. a knife is made to cut, humans are made to be kind, sexuality is for companionship, sexual satisfaction and procreation and as preparation for the loving, universal relationships of the City of God, a bit like trainer wheels on childrens' bikes.

A secondary reason for rejecting homosexual practice (not persons) is that it is fruitless or non-procreational, frustrating part of the natural purpose of our bodily sexuality, as Greco-Roman natural law and its Catholic varieties recognise. But Genesis 2:23 does not mention

---

44.   Following O'Donovan "The Natural Ethic," 19-25.

procreation as primary. Adam cries with joy, "This at last is bone of my bones and flesh of my flesh; she shall be called Woman, for from man she was taken." Adam doesn't say "This at last is big hips for child-bearing and big breasts for child-feeding!" Nor does Paul mention procreation as his main reason for rejection of homosexual practice in Romans 1:24-27, even though it was an urgent imperative in ancient society and soon will be in many western societies with less than replacement population rates.

This basic biblical idea of sexual ecology is supported by gay health activist Gabriell Rotello's book *Sexual Ecology* (though Rotello does not reject homosexual practice). He bravely challenges various gay myths which are killing gays, especially "the pervasive myth that humans have somehow transcended the limits of the biological world." Rotello argues that "the highly selective spread of HIV around the world shows that AIDS is … an ecological epidemic that exploits certain behaviours, … the single riskiest sexual practice of all: anal sex."[45]

While recognising some usefulness of safe sex campaigns and condoms, Rotello rightly challenges sole reliance on "the condom code" as "anti-ecological", a classic "technological fix." The church and wider community have relied on consequences alone for too long.[46] Rotello's argument is "rooted not in traditional morality, but implacable biology." But unless the moral and biological are arbitrarily separated, the logic of his argument leads towards a moral version of sexual or "moral ecology."[47] In this way, Rotello's logic supports my argument that biology and ecology back up the Bible. God's two books, Scripture and nature, in that order, agree.

(London: Plume, 1998), 188.

46. Rotello, 8-10, 187. Though consequences do have a rightful place in Patrick Dixon, *The Rising Price of Love: The True Cost of the Sexual Revolution* (London: Hodder & Stoughton, 1995).

47. See Michael Novak, "Awakening from Nihilism," *First Things* (August/September 1994), 18-22 and *The Catholic Ethic and the Spirit of Capitalism* (New York: Free Press, 1993), 215-37. Cf. John Paul II, *Centesimus Annus* no. 50.

2. Knowing Creation/Nature after the Fall

Well before postmodernity, Emil Brunner recognised this created ecology—"the world is not a shapeless mass of matter, it is not a chaos which we have to reduce to form and order. It was formed long ago ... in a rich variety of form ... In its form the will of God is stamped upon that which exists."[48] The world is a God-shaped cosmos, for Brunner, not a chaos awaiting us to redraw the sexual wheel.

Yet how do we discern what is divine order and what is human disorder? Michel Foucault claims that notions of natural and unnatural are historically, socio-culturally and politically constructed and that almost any cultural and institutional configuration of pleasure can be constructed and depicted as natural.[49] Theological "postmodernists" like Stanley Hauerwas rightly note that "appeals to creation too often amount to legitimating strategies for the principalities and powers that determine our lives," leading us to project our present "twilight of good and evil" onto the canvas/screen of creation.[50] They cite the misuse of the doctrine of the orders of creation to justify Nazi racism and by some contemporary Christians to justify sexism or homophobia.

This misuse of arguments from nature has led to the near rejection of creation as part of the Christian master-narrative or the idea of a master narrative at all, as justifying the mastery of some over others.[51] Yet James Gustafson correctly sees Hauerwas abandoning the distinction between right use and abuse of nature. Thus "Nature is ... of no ethical significance as a source of direction in Hauerwas's

---

48.   *The Divine Imperative* (London: Lutterworth Press, 1937), 124-25.

49.   Michel Foucault, *History of Sexuality,* vol 1, Introduction (Pantheon, New York: 1978), 105. Cf. J.J. Winkler, *The Constraints of Desire: The Anthropology of Sex and Gender in Ancient Greece* (New York: 1990), 17.

50.   *Dispatches from the Front: Theological Engagements with the Secular* (Durham NC: Duke University Press, 1994), 111. Despite Hauerwas' disavowal of the label "postmodernist," he is so here.

51.   See Pim Pronk, *Against Nature: Types of Moral Argumentation* (Grand Rapids: Eerdmans, 1993).

ethics. Hauerwas becomes a twentieth-century version of Marcion."[52] Similarly, much postmodern theology is now "an Omega that has no Alpha", an end without a beginning.[53] This is true of the whole of *FUP*, which lacks a creation-based foundation, starting in mid-air. But it is particularly so of Peta Sherlock's chapter on Romans 1:26-27 which relativises away what Paul says about nature as some kind of Stoic cultural commentary, instead of attempting to depict God's transcultural creation.[54]

We agree with Sherlock that the interpretative crux of Paul's attack on homosexual practice are these words. Peta sees this reflecting "the conventional Stoic sense of "nature" as the established order of things" (cf Romans 11:21, 24 on the natural Jewish olive branches). Paul is condemning lustful heterosexuals turning against their own sexual nature by acting as homosexuals. Paul has "no understanding of people who are genuinely or 'naturally' homosexual." Romans 1:26-27, in her view, says nothing about a homosexual couple in a faithful, committed and loving relationship.[55]

As Sherlock says, context is crucial. Rather than the distant Romans 11:21, 24, much nearer is Romans 1:20. Here Paul talks from about the cosmic context of creation/nature, of idolaters worshipping the creature not the Creator. Homosexual acts are a symptom of idolatry and God's judgment, by turning from created truth to lies while lying with the same-sex. It is not about a subjective view of

---

52. James Gustafson, "A Response to Critics," *Journal of Religious Ethics* 13 (1985), 191 cited in Michael Banner, *Christian Ethics and Contemporary Problems* (Cambridge University Press, 1999), 20. He notes that Gustafson should speak more theologically of "creation" not "nature." Despite Stanley Hauerwas' *With the Grain of the Universe: The Church's Witness and Natural Theology* (London: SCM, 2002) he still, like Barth, confuses our subjective epistemological difficulty of accessing the created order and its objective ontology, cf. "'Capitalism' and Why Gays (as a group) are Morally Superior to Christians (as a group)" in *Dispatches* ch. 6.

53. As Hans Urs von Balthasar said, cited by Banner, *Christian Ethics* 19.

54. "Reading Romans as Anglicans: Romans 1:26-27," *Five Uneasy Pieces: Essays on Scripture and Sexuality* (Adelaide: ATF Press, 2011), 41.

55. "Reading Romans," 41-42.

our individual sexual nature, what's in our *mind,* but our created *kind,* male and female, nor about a cultural view of socio-political order. He is clearly talking about the created order, natural law or 'sexual ecology'.

Further, the highly cosmopolitan Paul was likely also aware of Greco-Roman views of various homosexual relationships, including consenting, monogamous and life-long ones.[56] Paul's terms and examples, including lesbians, uniquely, include the widest range of homosexual acts. Paul is against homosexual practice as turning upside down our sexual ecology of complementarity, equality and unity. It is against the transcultural created order based on Genesis 1:26-28 when male and female were made in God's image.

Sherlock sees no transcultural norm for sexual behaviour—"Could it be that Scripture encourages us to live without unequivocal guidance about most sexual matters?"[57] For her "All you need is love." But in a world of "Liquid Love" this is an easy, parochial accommodation to the gay culture of western postmodern cities, an accommodation that many Christians are uneasy with, due to the uneasiness we feel spiritually and pastorally about the plight of homosexual victims of a sexually idolatrous world.

The contemporary social location of such anti-creational views are found among the sexually expressive urban elites or cosmopolitan new middle class who can choose who, when, and where to relate to, and how. Sociologist David Reisman anticipated their looking down on "the provinciality of being born to a particular family in a particular

---

56. As Larry W. Hurtado, "The Bible and Same-Sex Erotic Relations," *Crux* (June 1996), Vol XXXII, No. 2, 19 says: "I must ... express doubts about claims that the ancient world knew nothing of consensual, caring, same-sex relationships or nothing of people whose sexual desires were exclusively same-sex. The ancient Greek evidence indicates otherwise." Hurtado rightly questions also the idea of a cultural creation out of nothing, as if modern cultures have generated a new phenomenon called homosexuality with so little to do with the ancient one that anything the Bible says is irrelevant. Bruce Thornton, *Eros: The Myth of Greek Sexuality* (Boulder: Westview, 1997) is an excellent survey.

57. "Reading Romans," 43.

place [and looking forward to the desired time] when ties based on *conscious relatedness* would replace those of blood and soil."[58]

As an expression of this rootless cosmopolitanism, yesterday's sociology, often justifying a particular academic and social location, regularly becomes today's theology. Liberal Catholic theologian J.J. McNeill is typical in going to the social constructionist extreme. He argues that:

> the call of the Gospel to man is not one of conforming passively to biological givens; rather that call is to transform and humanise the natural order through the power of love ... what it means to be a man or woman in any given society is a free human cultural creation.[59]

These noble sounding words are in fact a Gnostic rejection of creation or biology altogether. Likewise, former Uniting Church minister and continuing lesbian Dorothy McRae-McMahon, who resigned soon after "coming out," said, like many, "this is the way God created me." But this is an individualistic and subjective distortion of Luther's existential emphasis on 'God created *me*" in his *Shorter Catechism*. For theologians like the above (not Luther), creation "lacks any inherent good apart from this grasping and humanising,"[60] something any ecologist can recognise as very anthropocentric and arbitrary.

How do we tell if we have grasped this order well or badly without an ontological reference point? It is like trying to grasp a jellyfish, there's no backbone, structure or form to hold onto. We are left with vague values of "justice and love,"[61] which are loosely used to justify sex outside heterosexual marriage in many mainline liberal church sexuality reports.

---

58. David Reisman with Nathan Glazer and Reuel Denney, *The Lonely Crowd* (Hartford: Yale University Press, 1950), xlvii.

59. *The Church and the Homosexual* (Boston: Beacon, 1977), 102-4.

60. Banner, *Christian Ethics* 279.

61. McNeill, *The Church and the Homosexual* 148.

Yet, without a sense of "authoritative nature" it is difficult to deny the wrongness of paedophilia, bestiality or incest if such relationships are loving, non-painful, or consensual.[62] These practices may well be the next battlegrounds as some in the American Psychiatric Association want them recognised as harmless and delisted as disorders.

Postmodern social constructionism is fallacious like the projection theory of religious needs; just because we are hungry does not mean that food doesn't really exist. Further, just because people ideologically abuse the notion of the natural for their own power doesn't deny the existence of the natural. Abuse of the notion of creation order does not deny its use, it just disciplines our critical discernment of it, or we would do away with sex too, the most abused of all precious human goods.

We can reject reading natural laws simplistically from analogies to animals (e.g. monogamy from the documentary *The March of the Penguins*—pity it's only temporary) or from genitals being seen as only or primarily for procreation (pity about the clitoris) as unbiblical, un-holistic and impersonal. And we can reject wrong notions of the natural or biologism (biological determinism) without rejecting all notions of the natural or biological.

What we need is not to throw the baby of nature out with the bathwater of ideological constructions or deconstructions of it. Instead we need "a corrected account of creation; i.e. one which does not crassly identify what is the case with God's will for the world?"[63] This is known as critical realism: yes there are real universal truths/

---

62. Banner, *Christian Ethics* 272 n 5. A new Dutch single-issue political group seeks to legalise pedophilia. Australian philosopher Peter Singer supports (non-painful) bestiality. See Gordon Preece, *Rethinking Peter Singer* (Downers Grove: IVP, 2002), 23-26. Former Australian Governor-General, Bishop Peter Hollingworth notoriously suggested on ABC TV's *Australian Story* (2002) that the case of a 14 year old girl's sexual relationship with a priest, later bishop, was mitigated as consensual.

63. Banner, *Christian Ethics* 17. Cf. Robert Scharleman, *Happiness and Benevolence* (Edinburgh: T&T Clark, 2000) from a more Catholic, philosophical perspective affirming the teleology or goal of nature.

ideas, but we need to carefully and critically distinguish them from particular cultural, economic, class and gender ideologies.

A corrected account begins with three theological tenses of any narrative of nature:

1. Past—Edenic natural laws/ ideals of marriage including equality, complementarity and procreation between the sexes, which should no more be ignored than if we were to write a sex manual ignoring the laws of gravity;

2. Present—fallen nature (Gen 3 on) subject to futility and idolatry (Eccles, Rom 1:20 ff; 8:18 ff.) but being restored in Christ now;

3. Future—nature redeemed to reach its goal, for which it, our bodies and the Spirit groan with the pangs of the new creation like a mother in childbirth (Rom 8:18ff.).

In Matthew's Gospel Jesus enables us to see all three aspects of sexuality in response to the Pharisees' and Sadducees' questions regarding divorce and marriage in heaven:

1. God's original, created purpose—one man, one wife for life (19:3-6)

2. God's permissions, like divorce, for hardness of heart (19:7-9)

3. Celibacy or "eunuchs for the sake of the kingdom" (19:12). "For in the resurrection they neither marry nor are given in marriage, but are like angels in heaven" (22:30 NRSV as are all biblical references unless noted).

In correcting the Pharisees' desire for "anything goes" divorce, Christ took them not to our heavenly end, but back to the beginning, to God's creational purpose of one man, one wife, for life (Mt 19:1-12). Despite the cliché that Jesus said nothing about homosexuality (a logically suspect argument from silence), he upheld Genesis' view of heterosexual marriage. Matthew 19 is a crucial Christological and Gospel span between the Law of Creation in Genesis and the Epistle to Romans to which we turn. This provides the broad canonical canvas on which "the small number of texts' on homosexuality are written and read.

Because of the Fall's disruption to the natural order and our ability to know it (Rom 1:18-32) the Bible and Augustine leave sexuality not "merely to the endless rhythms of nature" but incorporate it into the redemptive rhythm of creation, fall and redemption. John Calvin and Karl Barth follow Augustine here. For Barth, the ethical question regarding sex is "essentially a question of things that are natural and right," but not "securely naturally known."[64] Our access to the natural is revelational. Calvin describes how Scripture puts glasses on us to see creation's scattered signs clearly.[65]

Biblical revelation of our being made in God's image enables us to see sexuality's personal and relational aspects. This can be seen against the background of a perverted form of naturalism which absolutises nature as it is now, fallen nature—not natural law, but natural flaw.[66] An example is the aptly named The Bloodhounds songline:"you and me baby aint nothing but mammals, let's do it like they do on the Discovery Channel." Another example is that infamous collector of wasps and deviant sexual behaviours from unrepresentative prison and university student populations, Alfred Kinsey.[67]

Instead of being a form of sexual solitaire and animalistic stimulation, sex is an expression of our personal, relational nature

---

64. *Church Dogmatics (CD) III/4, 120.*

65. "For as the aged, or those whose sight is defective, when any book, however fair, is set before them, though they perceive that there is something written, are scarcely able to make out two consecutive words, but, when aided by glasses, begin to read distinctly, so Scripture, gathering together the impressions of Deity, which, till then, lay confused in our minds, dissipates the darkness, and shows us the true God clearly" *Institutes I vi.1.* http://www.ccel.org/ccel/calvin/institutes.iii.vii.html accessed 5/2/12.

66. See Bruce S. Thornton, *Eros: The Myth of Greek Sexuality* (Boulder: Westview Press, 1997), 7 on Greek ambivalence or negativity about nature as something to be controlled, if possible, by culture.

67. See Judith A. Reisman and Edward W. Eichel, *Kinsey, Sex and Fraud: The Indoctrination of a People* eds. J Gordon Muir and John H. Court (Lafayette, La: Huntington House, 1990) and James H. Jones, *Alfred C Kinsey* (New York: W.W Norton, 1998) which show Kinsey as a bisexual, voyeur, exhibitionist, and masochist.

as men and women made in God's relational, trinitarian image. This God is the ground and goal of our identity, whether we are married or single.[68] When the two become one there is a mysterious image of that trinitarian oneness in difference, where there is a basic complementarity and completeness, unity and non-competitive equality (Gen 2:24, Mt 19:5, Eph 5:28-33).

In Romans 1:24 ff. Paul depicts homosexual practice as a symptom of Gentile idolatry and God's giving them up to disordered and unnatural desires. In Romans 7:13-25 Paul graphically describes the Adamic self (still existing within the Christian) divided by all-demanding desire, including sexual desire. Following Paul, Augustine partially deconstructed the Greeks' Olympian harmonious soul-body dualism. Autobiographically in his *Confessions*, he explored humanity's broken sexuality in a much more fundamental way than any postmodern de-centering or fragmentation of the self. Augustine found its source in the Pauline 'dissociation of body, reason and will."[69] This leads to a disordering of our now competing loves and desires. Desires become demands, captive to the law of sin competing with the mind/conscience's recognition of the goodness of God's law.[70]

According to Romans 1:20 ff.—anarchic or disordered, anonymous or depersonalised desire flows from idolatry. Idolatry means worshipping the creature, including sex, not the Creator. It makes good things into gods. As Augustine notes, the basic problem of the earthly city is that it does not do justice to God's worth, by refusing to worship him, and by sacrificing to other gods. One of the most powerful of these gods in Augustine's and our age, is clearly Eros, the god of sex.

---

68.   Barth, *CD III/2*.

69.   Banner, *Christian Ethics* 298 citing Augustine, *Confessions, Book viii* 10, 22.

70.   Francis Watson, *Agape and Eros: Pauline Sexual Ethics* (Cambridge: Cambridge University Press), 2000 cf. Paul Ramsey, "Human Sexuality in the History of Redemption," *Journal of Religious Ethics 16* (1988), 56.

3. Redemptive Therapy and Creation Healed

The biblical story of "the Kingdom of God is creation healed,"[71] the source of complete sexual liberation and wholeness. Healing powers radiate out from the city of God which has within it the tree of life "for the healing of the nations" (Rev 22:2). Redemptive ethics or therapy buys back creation by re-channeling our sexuality within creaturely limits. This demythologises the modern sexual liberationist and consumerist myth that allows uncontrolled, covetous desire to flood every part of life. In this redemptive way eros or desire is healed and made part of the whole of Christ's sacrificial love or agape. Only the love of the crucified and resurrected Christ can liberate us from this body of deathly, disordered desire because his love is stronger than death.

Though intimately related to identity, sexuality, whether hetero-, homo-, or bi-sexuality, is not to be idolatrously equated with our identity. Sexuality is not the soul or the whole of a person, though it has taken over its role in modernity. But if our sexuality is not the basis of our identity, then sex will not save, or bring wholeness. National Gay and Lesbian Task Force (NGLTF) executive director Torie Osborne summed up the more sober post-AIDS view of some:

> The radicals won the "sex wars," but we lost the truly radical vision of full human liberation in the process. The idea of sex as salvation and as self, which dominates gay male—and now young lesbian—culture [and many straights], holds no promise for real change; it is consumeristic and ultimately hollow.[72]

Sexuality does not provide the transcendent liberation many seek. People mistake the sign for the reality it signifies or points to. Instead, sexuality is a sign or sacrament of relationship with a trinitarian relational God. Sexuality and its stabilisation in marriage is a sign or metaphor of God's propositioning us, God's marrying his people, in an exclusive, intimate, purifying relationship (Hosea, Eph

---

71. Hans Kung, *On Being a Christian* translated by Edward Quinn (London, UK: William Collins, 1977), 231.

72. In her *Advocate* column in late 1994 cited in Rotello, *Sexual Ecology* 288.

5:21ff, Rev 21:1, 2). Unlike modern romantic myths, this is a realistic, robust romance that can re-enchant cynical postmodern sexuality.[73]

This corporate view of the body and of bodily church discipline on sexual issues appears harsh to individualistic modern Christians. But the early church had no concrete signs such as the sabbath, circumcision or food laws to maintain its distinctiveness like its Jewish parent/brother. One of its primary signs or practices was its bodily discipline or heightened sexual ethic, which set it apart as a holy people, a third race.[74]

> Modern Christians who feel that traditional Christianity attached undue importance to sexual morality and made it too restrictive need to be aware that their own lack of sympathy with the traditional discipline arises not only from sexual liberation but also from a different ecclesiology, from a lowering of boundaries between the Church and the world. The broad questions of the ... precise sense in which the Christian should be in the world but not of it, need to be ... resolved before the sexual ethic of traditional Christianity can be rightly understood and fairly judged.[75]

Paul and the early church engaged in a form of Christian social and political construction which we need to recapture our integrity and distinctiveness as the body of Christ. When Christian bodies engage sexually with other bodies they do so first and foremost as members of the body of Christ.[76] In a world of *The Clash of Civilizations* and *Global*

---

73.   Cf. Charles Williams, *An Outline of Romantic Theology: Religion and Love in Dante* ed. Alice Mary Hadfield (Grand Rapids: Eerdmans, 1990), and James Wm. McClendon Jr, *Ethics: Systematic Theology vol. I* (Nashville: Abingdon), 1986, ch. 5 "The Romance of Orthodoxy."

74.   Richard M. Price, "The Distinctiveness of Early Christian Sexual Ethics," in A. Thatcher and E. Stuart ed. *Christian Perspectives on Sexuality and Gender* (Herefordshire/Grand Rapids: Gracewing/Eerdmans, 1996), 29. Cf. Peter Brown, *The Body and Society: Men, Women and Sexual Renunciation in Early Christianity* (New York: Columbia University Press, 1988), ch 1 and Epilogue, esp. 428.

75.   Price, "Distinctiveness," 29.

76.   See Dale Martin, *The Corinthian Body* (New Haven: Yale University Press, 1995) for background on Paul's semi-medical view of sexual pollution,

Sex[77] we need to think how the body of Christ can regain a notion of nurturing discipleship of and discipline over the bodies of Christians.

The real contest today is between Third World Christianity and Islam. Western Christianity is too flabby and weak to be in the contest. It is no accident that the growing churches were those leading the way for sexual purity at the Lambeth Anglican Bishops Congress in 1998. The African bishops were not only biblical, but preventatively pastoral with an eye on their massive AIDS crisis, and missiological concerning Muslims who see Christianity as accommodated to a sexually decadent West. We should share their concern, and not parochially sell out our sexual ethics to inner-city westerners, while still seeking to be hospitable to them.

The really difficult issue though, is how to recapture a thick or strong enough community or church life to model committed Christ-like relationships for younger people under much pressure to conform sexually. Like the Ancient Greeks we need to mentor and apprentice young people into mature, sexual adulthood and citizenship of the city or polis—not in pederastic, homosexual style, as some wrongly claim they advocated,[78] but into citizenship of the city of God, an even higher good than the created good of sexuality.

The eroticisation of everyday life has caused the sad decline of non-sexual opposite-sex friendship and cast suspicion on same-sex friendships. We need to recover a range of committed, even covenantal relationships, such as marriage and parenthood, and same-sex non-sexual friendships like Jonathan and David, Ruth and Naomi. These could help meet the need for intimacy, even a "holy kiss" (1 Cor 16:20), but not genital intimacy, unless heterosexually married.[79]

---

although he reads Paul unsympathetically.

77. Samuel Huntington, *The Clash of Civilizations and the Remaking of World Order* (New York: Simon & Schuster, 1997) and Denis Altman, *Global Sex* (St. Leonards: Allen & Unwin, 2001).

78. See Eva Cantarella, *Bisexuality in the Ancient World* (New Haven: Yale University Press, 1992) and contrast Thornton, *Eros,* 256-7.

79. On same-sex friendship see Michael Vasey, *Strangers and Friends: A New*

Richard Hays provides a poignant depiction cf his own intimate friendship with his late gay friend Gary. He depicts non-practising homosexuals who struggle with their sexuality as heroes of the faith, caught as they are between the now and not yet of the kingdom, awaiting the redemption of their bodies. 'Straight' Christians should provide wherever possible, comfort and companionship on the way to the resurrection of the body of all believers, straight and gay, into the new creation and city of God.[80]

3.1. Sexual Liberation—Back to the Naked Garden or Forward to God's City?

Paul's realistic narrative and eschatological theology is foreign to many contemporary family values advocates' quest for heaven through family, and also to many sexual liberals' quest for an Eden of free sexual expression. The Woodstock generation sang their anthem along with Joni Mitchell and Crosby, Stills, Nash and Young: "We are stardust, we are golden, we are billion year old carbon, and we've got to get ourselves back to the garden" as they romped naked in rain and mud, like Israel before the Golden Calf (1 Cor 10:6-8). Sex was seen as salvation, paradise, the garden of Eden.

Gabriell Rotello adopts a more realistic ecological and cultural perspective. He says: "Deep ecology recognises that our thoughts, beliefs, and social systems are as much a part of nature's web as any other factor in ecology" and "require fundamental changes in human

---

Exploration of Homosexuality (London: Hodder & Stoughton, 1995); Stanley Hauerwcs, "Gay Friendship: A Thought Experiment in Catholic Moral Theology," in his Sanctify them in the Truth: Holiness Exemplified (Edinburgh: T&T Clark, 1998), ch. 6, and Peter Carnley's chapter in The Doctrine Panel of General Synod, Faithfulness in Fellowship: Reflections on Homosexuality and the Church (Melbourne: John Garret, 2001). However, Carnley smuggles the meaning of marriage into gay friendships to avoid confrontation over gay marriages and the association of marriage with procreation. Theologically the primary problem is lack of sexual complementarity and for many gays the basic problem is monogamy.

80. Richard B. Hays, "Awaiting the Redemption of our Bodies," Sojourners (July 1991), 17-21.

organization and philosophy" if we want "sustainable solutions."[81] Contrary to the notion of gay sex as historically unchangeable, the relatively recent gay gym culture with its incredible discipline over the body shows how cultural discipline can bring change.[82] Rotello wants to restore the more Greek type of spiritualised, self-controlled sex[83] through social incentives encouraging universally recognised monogamy. But for all his positive health proposals for gays, Rotello is a moral relativist. He fails to reckon with Bruce Thornton's demonstration that the Greek form of therapy for erratic eros was *heterosexual* marriage.

Theologians too can mimic a seventies romanticism about sexual liberation. James Nelson, whose books were eagerly cited by many mainline liberal sexual reports in the nineties, wrote *Between Two Gardens*. But Nelson is utterly utopian in thinking that sex now is unambiguously good, with no flaming sword blocking our way back to the garden of pure sexual delight. He highlights the idyllic romanticism of the garden in Song of Songs over the fallen garden of Eden in Genesis 3 with its tension between the innocence and ambiguity of sex. Nelson has no sense of the eschatological end of sex, no sense of the garden's goal within the city of God, and therefore no reason for sexual restraint.[84]

On the other hand, Peta Sherlock charges us to "interpret from heaven backwards, not creation forwards."[85] But in pushing new creation at the expense of creation she forgets that it is not another creation out of nothing. It is new in the sense of a restored creation, like Michelangelo's Sistine Chapel in full glorious colour, which I saw twenty years after my first glimpse of its somewhat greyed overlay of centuries of discolouration.

---

81.   Rotello, *Sexual Ecology,* 187-8.

82.   Rotello, 254, 299-300.

83.   Rotello, 225-27.

84.   See James Nelson, *Between Two Gardens* (New York: Pilgrim, 1983), 7-9.

85.   Sherlock, "Reading Romans," 38.

Sherlock notes that Jesus tells the Sadducees that contrary to popular myth there's no marriage in heaven (Mk 12:18-27), for marriage is "till death us do part." Heterosexual marriage is good but not God, it is for a time, not eternal. Sherlock resorts to quoting Paul's "we see in a mirror dimly" now (1 Cor 13:12) to cast doubt on such bodily continuity. But therefore to understand heaven, our best bets or biblically educated hunches are based on creation and Christ's restoration of creation. The Alpha or beginning and Omega or end must be held together in Christ.

Much of the liberal utopian sexual agenda sees our sexuality as our property, in an externalised, almost capitalistic sense, where costs or violations of our sexual ecology are externalised or hidden. Free use of our sexual property is merely limited by the rights of others, rather than being part of our person. It shows a Pelagian[86] naivety about human nature and unfettered, neutral freedom, limitless liberty, as if each sinful act is atomistic with no long chain of after-effects. It assumes that a utopian view of the sexual body as ongoing incarnational sexual revelation,[87] plus a bit of sexual therapy and technique, will solve all our sexual problems.

Sadly, we have replaced the biblical and Augustinian city of God with the modern Enlightenment quest for the Heavenly City on earth, originally through reason, increasingly through sexual passion. As Foucault says:

> A great sexual sermon—which has had its subtle theologians and its popular voices—has swept through our societies over the last decades; it has chastised the old order [of Christian and Victorian repression] and denounced hypocrisy and praised the rights of the immediate and real; it has made people dream of a New City.[88]

---

86. Pelagius (ca. AD 354—ca. AD 420/440) was a British monk opposed to Augustine's robust view of sin and the necessity of grace.

87. James Nelson, *Body Theology* (Louisville: WJKP, 1992), 9. Contrast Linda Woodhead, "Sex in a Wider Context," in Jon Davies and Gerard Loughlin eds. *Sex These Days* (Sheffield Academic Press: 1997), 102-3.

88. *The History of Sexuality vol. 1* trans. Robert Hurley, (New York: Vintage

People seeking this New City foolishly think of it as a god-like *creatio ex nihilo,* out of nothing, as if God did not create order in the first place. Like an erratic jazz musician, they seek to culturally and sexually improvise without any created rhythm to improvise upon.[89] Yet "the word 'culture' comes originally from agriculture [cf. Gen 2:15]; culture is nature humanised, not abrogated."[90]

In the end, all impurity or lack of created wholeness will be cast out of the city of God, the truly urbane, humane city. Allow me to use an imperfect analogy to illustrate.[91] The first time I visited Times Square, New York with my wife in the early 1980s, it was known aptly as Hell's Bedroom. It was full of prostitutes and intimidating pimps. We were scared and got out of there ASAP, not even going to Broadway. The second time we went was 1997. The transformation was astonishing. The city centre had been cleaned up and we felt safe walking the streets at midnight with teenage children. This transformed city is a reminder of the city on which all who trust in God have their hope set, a city which could also inspire many Christians in their efforts to challenge not only the private bedrooms but also the public boardrooms of our culture.

Conclusion

I conclude and summarise with a final image of how the Bible and Augustine reframe our sexual story in the light of creation and re-creation. Rembrandt's painting "Bathsheba" below uses a similar creation, fall, redemption framework, characteristic of Rembrandt,

---

Books, 1980), 7-9.

89.   Dietrich Bonhoeffer calls this a *"cantus firmus"* or "ground bass" in God's incarnate in Christ love holding all our polyphonous human loves together. *Letters and Papers from Prison* (London: SCM, 1953), 99-100. Contrast this with Richard Holloway's use of jazz as a model for moral improvisation in his *Godless Morality: Keeping Religion Out Of Ethics* (Canongate: 1999).

90.   Spaemann, *Happiness and Benevolence* 167. Cf. C. Westermann, *Creation* (London: SPCK, 1971).

91.   The analogy is imperfect as the prostitutes and homeless were excluded by zero tolerance policing.

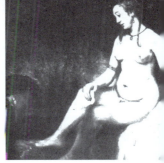

over against the classical legacy of the city of Rome.[92] The beautiful, naked Bathsheba reflects the created glory of the human body bathed in golden light. But she wears the melancholy look of the Fall and shame at her nakedness before the distant gaze of the adulterous King David high on the hill. Also unnoticed by her, perhaps, is "a figure who attends her as she bathes, washing her feet, one who will later be borne of her genealogy" (Mt 1:6-7), one who came to serve (Lk 22:27) and clean our feet, indeed our whole selves, with the complete cleansing of the cross (Jn 13). "Thus the light that falls on Bathsheba is not only the light of Eden, but the light of the 'holy city' the new Jerusalem."[93] It is this light, this cleansing that we need for the New York of *Sex and the City*, the archetypal postmodern city, and for our morose postmodern sexual mores, heterosexual and homosexual.

92.   Kenneth Clark, *Introduction to Rembrandt* (London: Icon, 1978), 115.

93.   Benner, *Christian Ethics* 308-9 who pointed me to Clark and Rembrandt's *Bathsheba*.

CHAPTER 2

Let Sodom be Sodom! Another Look at Genesis 19

LINDSAY WILSON

> But before they lay down, the men of the city, the men of Sodom, both young and old, all the people to the last man, surrounded the house; and they called to Lot, "Where are the men who came to you tonight? Bring them out to us, so that we may know them." (Gen 19:4-5 NRSV)

The account of Sodom's sin in Genesis 19 is *not* one of the pivotal passages used in developing a traditioncl and evangelical understanding of homosexuality. It is not entirely irrelevant, as we shall see, but it is certainly not the lynchpin. However, since the volume *Five Uneasy Pieces* has included a discussion of Sodom by Megan Warner, it is appropriate to re-examine the text and context of Genesis 19 in response to her chapter. The strength of Warner's contribution (one of the best in the book) is that it is seeking to grapple with the text and its meaning, and this study shall seek to do likewise.

What Did Go On In Sodom?

The identification of Sodom's sin is the heart of the issue raised by Warner. In the light of some recent scholarship, should we still conclude that homosexuality is an issue in the Sodom narrative, or is there a better way to read these texts? Is it only about inhospitality and violence, or is homosexual practice also condemned? This is a worthwhile issue to raise, and many of Warner's observations are helpful, but in the end she does not provide a convincing way of interpreting and applying this passage.

Genesis 19 has traditionally been approached on the basis that at least part of the sin of Sodom is male hcmosexual activity. The men of Sodom ask Lot to bring out the two "men" so that they may "know" them, usually understood to mean "have (homo)sex with" them. Their sins are elsewhere described in more general terms, such as in Genesis 13:13 ("the men of Sodom were wicked, great sinners") and 18:20-21 ("the outcry against Sodom and Gomorrah is great and their sin is very grave"). But it is the incident in 19:1-11, in which the men of Sodom demand to "know" the two men in Lot's house, that provides the most specific details.

Of course, other wrongs than sexual sin are clearly included in the wickedness of Sodom. One sin often leads to others. The word "outcry" in Genesis 18:20 is commonly associated with injustice, so that was likely to be a problem in Sodom. The demand that Lot surrender the two men in his house touches on the sins of inhospitality and violence as well as any sexual wrongdoing.

Sodom in the Rest of Scripture

Some seek to solve this dilemma by an appeal to how other scriptural texts interpret this passage. Warner makes the interesting claim that "there is no text in the Hebrew Bible (Old Testament), other than Genesis 19 itself, in which the populace of Sodom is connected with a reputation for homosexuality or any other kind of sexual behaviour."[94] Building on Brett, she cites the way that Sodom is picked up in the OT prophetic texts (e.g. Isa 1:10; 3:9; Jer 23:14; Ezek 16:49) and argues that the essential sin of Sodom was the unjust oppression of the weak.[95] However, while Ezekiel 16:46-50 suggests that pride or injustice was rampant in the city, it also refers to the "abominations" of the Sodomites. This term "abomination" is not used for the other sins identified in Sodom but is used in Leviticus 18:22 to refer to homosexual intercourse.[96]

Those taking the opposite side look instead at NT passages like Jude 7 and 2 Peter 2:6-10. Jude 7 is usually understood to claim that Sodom and Gomorrah were guilty of sexual immorality and the pursuit of unnatural desire. This is probably also the case, but not as clearly so in 2 Peter 2:6-10.

However, both of the arguments are methodologically weak because they do not look at the text of Genesis first. The issue at stake is not what parts of the Sodom tradition later readers focused on; it is rather, "what was the issue at stake in the narrative

94.   M. Warner, "Were the Sodomites Really Sodomites? Homosexuality in Genesis 19," in *Five Uneasy Pieces: Essays on Scripture and Sexuality* (Adelaide: ATF, 2011), 6.

95.   Warner, "Sodomites," 5, citing M.G. Brett, *Genesis: Procreation and the Politics of Identity* (London: Routledge, 2000).

96.   So S.J. Grenz, *Welcoming But Not Affirming* (Louisville: Westminster John Knox, 1998), 39.

in Genesis 19 itself?" The Sodom tradition is clearly picked up elsewhere in the Old and New Testaments, as is the story of Adam, the fall, Abraham and many others. But the proper hermeneutical approach is to read the narrative first in its own right, noticing its concerns, endorsements and warnings, rather than to retrofit it from later applications of the story. This is so whether the later writers connect Sodom with sexual immorality and unnatural desire (so Jude 7), or with the abuse of power (so Isaiah, Jeremiah and Ezekiel).

A Multiplicity of Sins?

Another option is that there was a multiplicity of sins in Sodom, and later texts referred primarily to those which were most relevant to their own context. Thus, the reference to widespread social injustice implied by the great outcry in Genesis 18:20, may have been of particular significance for prophets like Isaiah, Jeremiah and Ezekiel. There may have been sexual sin behind Genesis 18's description of Sodom (such as the term "abomination" in Ezekiel 16:47, 50), but Sodom seems to have been a champion of many sins.

Genesis 19, however, might be describing other sins prevalent in Sodom, such as breaches of hospitality and (homo)sexual sin. The particular circumstances of 19:1-11 involve a more specific and identified sin than those alluded to in chapter 18. Indeed, it is likely that the reason for the destruction of the city planned in Genesis 18 is for a wider range of sins than those outlined in chapter 19. Along these lines, Salier notes that "the city was destroyed not on account of the specific behaviour of its people towards Lot's guests, but because of habitual gross wickedness epitomised by their behaviour on this occasion."[97]

While the later prophetic references to Sodom pick up the descriptions of chapter 18, the focus in Jude and perhaps 2 Peter is more on the detail of chapter 19. In any event, the key to understanding the nature of the "wickedness" in 19:7 is to take a closer reading of the details of chapter 19 before reading it through the lens of either later OT or NT texts.

---

97. W.S. Salier, "Homosexuality and the Biblical Norm," *Evangelical 2* (1984): 84.

Genesis 2 as a Crucial Context for Genesis 19

One of the difficulties of the book *Five Uneasy Pieces* is its selection of passages. Choosing to start with Genesis 19 is itself a loaded choice. The implication is that this is the first place where the Old Testament has anything to say that might affect our understanding of homosexuality. However, Genesis 19 is part of the wider patriarchal account (Gen 12–50), which is a God-generated response to his dealings with all of creation in Genesis 1–11. This creational context (especially Gen 1–3) is indispensable for a right understanding of any aspect of sexuality.

Indeed, homosexuality is a subset of the broader category of the sexuality of all human beings. God's attitude towards homosexual people and actions must be seen as part of his understanding of humanity, made male and female in the image of God, entrusted as steward over the earth, and made for relationships with each other and with God. Genesis 2 in particular sets out the foundations of sexuality and relationship, by outlining the nature of a suitable, equal helper and the shape of that relationship. God's pattern for humanity consists of one woman and one man living together exclusively as one flesh. This is the nature of marriage, and would rule out, among other possibilities, a same-sex (male-male or female-female) marriage. The phrase "one flesh" implies that such a relationship is the proper context for sexual intimacy, and this is later made explicit for both Israel (e.g. Lev 18) and the church (e.g. 1 Cor 7). Thus, Warner's claim that "nowhere else in the book of Genesis is any concern expressed about homosexual activity" is dangerously half-true.[98] Since Genesis 2 outlines the context and parties for appropriate sexual activity, this has significant implications for homosexual activity.

The context of Genesis 2 cannot be ignored in coming to a view about homosexuality today. It is the setting of the biblical story, and its principles must be assumed in subsequent narratives, such as Genesis 19. When Jesus was asked about divorce (Matt

---

98.   Warner, "Sodomites," 3.

19:3-12), he did not simply pronounce on the topic of divorce itself. Instead, he put divorce in the context of marriage, and derived his understanding of marriage from the Genesis 2 creation account (Matt 19:4-6). Merely focusing on those passages mentioning divorce would not give a fully-biblical view of divorce, for divorce would be considered outside of its proper context of what the Bible teaches about marriage. So too with the issue of homosexuality. By the time the reader comes to Genesis 19, it is assumed that they have adopted the creation principles of Genesis 2. This includes understanding homosexual activity as contrary to God's purposes for humanity.

Barry Webb, for example, reminds us that the incident recorded in this chapter falls against the backdrop of the earlier material in Genesis and is evidence of further disorder in human relationships that resulted from the initial human rebellion [99] Richard Hays also acknowledges the need to read it in context. He points out that "From Genesis 1 onwards, scripture affirms repeatedly that God has made man and woman for one another and that our sexual desires rightly find fulfilment within heterosexual marriage ... This picture of marriage provides the positive backdrop against which the Bible's few emphatic negations of homosexuality must be read."[100]

The impression given in *Five Uneasy Pieces* is that the Bible only speaks about homosexuality in very few places.[101] However, once you realise the need for context, it is evident that the Bible speaks

---

99.   B.G. Webb, "Homosexuality in Scripture," in *Theological and Pastoral Responses to Homosexuality* (Adelaide: Openbook, 1994) 76. He concludes that the verb "to know" is most probably a demand for sex in Genesis 19:5, but believes that the focus overall is on homosexual rape rather than homosexuality per se.

100.   R. B. Hays, "Awaiting the Redemption of Our Bodies: The Witness of Scripture Concerning Homosexuality," in *Homosexuality in the Church: Both Sides of the Debate* ed. J.S. Siker (Louisville: Westminster John Knox, 1994), 10. This observation is even more significant since he argues that Genesis 19 is not relevant to "the morality of consensual homosexual intercourse."

101.   For example, Warner ("sodomites," 9) refers to "the small number of Biblical texts that address the subject of homosexuality."

about sexuality—and therefore homosexuality—at length, even devoting whole books to the subject (Song of Songs). It speaks about sex both positively (e.g. Prov 5:15-19) and negatively (e.g. Prov 7:25-27). It addresses those who are single (e.g. 1 Cor 7:8-9) and those who are married (e.g. 1 Cor 7:3-5). Whenever the Bible speaks about sexuality, this has implications for the issues of homosexuality, a point often overlooked by those who claim that Jesus says nothing on the topic of homosexuality.

In What Sense Do They Want to "Know" the Two Men (v. 5)?

One crucial key to understanding Genesis 19 is the meaning of the word "know" in verse 5. The Hebrew root *yada'* has a range of meanings from "acknowledge" to "know" to "have sexual relations with," and it is only the context which can determine which of these meanings is appropriate. While it has a range of meanings, that does not mean its meaning cannot be determined, and it is almost always clear from the surrounding context (e.g. Gen 4:1).

This brings us to the issue of whether the term "know" in verse 5 implies sexual activity.

Arguments Against the Traditional View

Doyle argues that *yada'* in Genesis 19:5 should be given "a neutral, non-sexual interpretation."[102] He notes that *yada'* is used 1058 times in the Hebrew Bible, only 15 of which refer to sexually knowing. He suggests that "given the statistical weight of the non-sexual usage of [dy [*yada"*], contextual evidence would seem to be indispensable in establishing a sexual reading of the term."[103] Since this common verb is used in a non-sexual sense in Genesis 18:19, 21, he proposes that it similarly has a non-sexual meaning in 19:5, 8. His conclusion is that "the people of Sodom were not out on a frenzied search for

---

102.   B. Doyle, "Knock, Knock, Knockin on Sodom's Door: The Function of tld/jtp in Genesis 18-19," 435. He is building on his earlier article, "The Sin of Sodom: *yada,* yada, yada: A Reading of the Mamre-Sodom Narrative in Genesis 18-19," *Theology and Sexuality* 9 (1998): 84-100.

103.   Doyle, "Knock, Knock," 436.

sexual gratification, their ultimate plan was "to know" the divine presence and thereby rise above the divine in an act of hubris."[104] On this view, the use of the verb in 19:8 does not provide the context for its meaning in v.5, and Lot is viewed as misunderstanding the intentions of the men of Sodom (v. 7).[105] He suggests that the men were not literally blinded, and he argues, implausibly, that they simply had an "inability to perceive," and have no right of access to the visitors.[106]

Warner also refers to some recent studies to suggest that the verb "know" might be in the context of a judicial enquiry—that they wish to know some facts about these men to see if their being offered hospitality would be a danger to the city itself. Thus, Morschauser proposes that the men of Sodom did not mean *yada'* in a sexual sense. Instead, they simply wanted to interrogate the visitors and determine whether or not they were spies, and that the offer of his daughters is simply Lot giving tokens of his good faith that he will send the men on their way in the morning. This is based on the phrase in Genesis 19:8 "to do good according to your eyes" (obscured in some translations) meaning assuming judicial responsibility.[107]

Along similar lines, Matthews argues that Lot did not have full citizenship in Sodom, and so he would not have the right to the sanctuary of hospitality.[108] He agrees with Morschauser that the confrontation is not based on the desire for sexual gratification and that Lot's offer of his daughters is not for sex, but is rather a legal gambit, offering them as hostages to the men of the city in return for securing the strangers' safety. This seems to override the

---

104. Doyle, "Knock, Knock," 438.

105. So, for example, Bechtel, as cited by Warner, "sodomites," 4.

106. Doyle, "Knock, Knock," 437-438.

107. S. Morschauser, "'Hospitality', Hostiles and Hostages: On the Legal Background to Genesis 19.1-19," *JSOT 27* (2003): 461-485.

108. V.H. Matthews, *More Than Meets the Ear: Discovering the Hidden Contexts of Old Testament Conversations* (Grand Rapids: Eerdmans, 2008) 147.

picture of Lot having a legitimate role in the legal and civic affairs of the city, signified by the phrase that "Lot was sitting in the gate of Sodom" (Gen 19:1). The gate to a city in the ANE was not merely the entrance, but the place where the leading men of a city decided the legal and public matters. For Lot to be taking his seat here implies a strong measure of belonging.

Both these views have their difficulties. At the very least, Doyle's view makes no sense of Lot's response, and can only read Lot as mistaken. This will be considered in the next section. Vandermeersch makes the interesting observation on Sherwin Bailey's seminal discussion of this incident (which is behind Doyle's view), asking that if Bailey is right that this passage has no application to contemporary homosexuality, why is there such stridency in arguing that the verb "to know" has no sexual connotation in Genesis 19?[109]

Morschauser's view may account for Lot's response, but does not resonate with the picture of Sodom given in the context. The picture which emerges from chapter 18 is not that Sodom was a place of sensible men carrying out judicious enquiries, but one of grave sin that led to an outcry for justice (Gen 18:20).

Arguments in Favour of the Traditional View

The arguments in favour of the traditional reading are much simpler. While the word "know" can simply mean that the men of Sodom wished to learn the identity of the two visitors, this does not account for the details of the story. These visitors had passed through the public entrance to the city, and spent some time in the main square dialoguing with Lot. If the men of Sodom wanted to know who they were, they had ample public opportunity.[110] Hamilton concludes that to think that all the Sodomites wanted was to become acquainted

---

109. P. Vandermeersch, "Sodomites, Gays and Biblical Scholars. A Gathering Organised by Peter Damian?," in *Sodom's Sins: Genesis 18-19 and its Interpretations* eds. E. Noort and E. Tigchelaar (Leiden: Brill, 2004), 157, 167.

110. So, G.J. Wenham, *Genesis 16-50* (WBC, Dallas: Word, 1994), 55.

with these visitors, "can only be evaluated as wild and fanciful."[111]

The traditional view can be supported by a number of details in the text and context.

Firstly, while the verb "know" most commonly has a non-sexual sense, it is frequently used in the book of Genesis to mean sexual intercourse. Wenham argues along these lines, and particularly notes that its use in verse 8 (Lot's daughters who had not "known" a man) clearly has this connotation, making it inescapable that it has a sexual meaning in verse 5.[112] Thus, both the wider and immediate context support the view that sexual intercourse with these visitors was an issue.

Secondly, the response of Lot is significant. Are we really meant to think that when Lot was asked whether they could talk to the messengers, he replied "no," but "here are my daughters for you to have sex with." That makes no narrative sense at all, or moral sense either. The story is clear that Lot understands their request to be for (homo)sexual intercourse with the two men in his house. Hamilton colourfully puts it like this: "the issue is intercourse not friendship. Lot would never have made such an unusual suggestion if the request was only for a handshake and moments of chitchat."[113]

Is it possible that Lot was mistaken, and has misled us ever since? Here we need to look again at the passage. Lot is not necessarily a model to be imitated. His choice of land in the valley has put himself and his family in physical and moral danger (Gen 13:10-13; 14:11-16; 18:20-21). His action of offering his daughters as a substitute

---

111. V.P. Hamilton, *The Book of Genesis Chapters 18-50* (NICOT, Grand Rapids: Eerdmans, 1995), 34.

112. Wenham, *Genesis 16-50*, 55; also Grenz, *Welcoming But Not Affirming* 37-38, who comments that "Even those who advocate a more open stance towards homosexuality find his [Sherwin Bailey's] exegesis suspect at this point." [i.e. in saying that it has nothing to do with sexuality, not even homosexual rape].

113. Hamilton, *Genesis 18-50*, 34.

is strongly questionable, even given some cultural differences.[114] This leads Webb to comment that "not only is Lot in Sodom but Sodom is in Lot."[115] However, he does show courage to put himself in the firing line, shutting the door behind him (19:6).

Yet, while he makes serious mistakes in the narrative, he is strongly portrayed here as being right to say no to the men of Sodom. All his actions may not be right, but this one certainly is. The two angelic visitors, acting for God in the story, reach out and protect Lot from the men of Sodom (19:10) and also strike the Sodomite mob with blindness (19:11). Regarding Lot as mistaken misinterprets the story, for it makes no sense of why the messengers had to blind the men of Sodom to thwart their plans (19:11). This seems to preclude the reading of Morschauser that the men of Sodom come with a legitimate legal question, and are entitled to have access to the visitors. Lot's stand against the men of Sodom is clearly endorsed in the chapter. He is not pictured as mistaken in his refusal to hand over the visitors. Presumably, he is also endorsed by the narrator when he describes the men of Sodom as "acting wickedly" (19:7). Letellier explores whether the intention of the men of Sodom could be viewed as innocent. He notes that "the manner in which Lot reacts, his anxiety that they should not sleep in the street, his action in standing between the door he has closed on his guests and the large, noisy crowd (v. 6) and his own reference to their evil intentions (v. 7), suggest otherwise."[116] He concludes that "the sexual nature of the Sodomites'" intentions can hardly be avoided in the context of Genesis 19."[117]

---

114.   So, Hamilton, *Genesis 18-50*, 36, who labels Lot's actions as "unconscionable," as inexcusable as the patriarchal attempts to pass off one's wife as one's sister.

115.   Webb, "Homosexuality in Scripture," 78.

116.   R.T. Letellier, *Day in Mamre, Night in Sodom: Abraham and Lot in Genesis 18 and 19* (BIS10, Leiden: Brill, 1995), 147.

117.   Letellier, *Day in Mamre, Night in Sodom* 157. He probably exceeds the evidence when he adds that "The perverse and specifically homosexual nature of their demands is underlined by their tacit and angry rejection of

Thirdly, the men of Sodom show that this is not a matter of an innocent and open enquiry. In verse 9, they say to Lot "we will deal worse with you than with them." The implication is that they had already decided how they would deal with the travellers. The men of Sodom were not just making innocent and legitimate legal inquiries about the two messengers. It seems that Lot correctly understood the nature of their demand.

There are, therefore strong grounds for retaining the view that the men of Sodom intended to have (homo)sexual intercourse with the two visitors, and that this is viewed as wickedness.

Homosexual Rape or Homosexual Sex?

Of course, Warner is right in pointing out that this may still only have rape rather than consensual sex in view, though she perhaps puts it too highly when she claims that "the story has nothing of any note to say about consensual sex between men."[118] This depends on whether Lot's description of their action as wicked (v.7) refers only to a breach of hospitality and the use of force, or whether it also has in view the crossing of a sexual boundary. In a recent "two sides of the debate" book, Dan Via argues that this chapter only condemns "homosexual gang rape." However, Robert Gagnon contends that the offence of the people of Sodom was "not just inhospitable rape of strangers," but there is also something wrong in the very action itself of this kind of sexual intercourse.[119] This requires us to take a deeper look at the nature of the sin(s) in this chapter.

---

the female substitutes (19,9)."

118.   Warner, "Sodomites," 3. Similarly, V.P. Furnish. "The Bible and Homsexuality: Reading the Texts in Context," in *Homosexuality in the Church: Both Sides of the Debate* ed. J.S. Siker (Louisville: Westminster John Knox, 1994) 18-35 at 19, and Dan Via in D.O. Via and R.J. Gagnon. *Homosexuality and the Bible: Two Views* (Minneapolis: Fortress, 2003), 5.

119.   Via and Gagnon, *Homosexuality and the Bible*, 5, 60.

What are the Sins of Sodom?

Clearly, the suggested action of the men of Sodom is wrong on several levels. If it involves forced rather than consensual sex, then it would be contrary to the mutuality and other-person-centredness of sexuality as it was designed by God to be. Loader suggests that the emphasis is on the social rather than sexual aspect of their sin. So, although sexual sin is part of what was being proposed, much more important was the "anti-social act of violence and oppression."[120] Forced sexuality (i.e. rape) is roundly and rightly condemned throughout scripture (e.g. Deut 22:25-29; 2 Sam 13:1-14). Lot would certainly find this violent aspect of their plan to be "wicked."

Furthermore, it is a breach of hospitality that would have been deeply shameful in that culture. Those of us who have grown up with Western values need to learn to read the Bible "through Middle Eastern eyes" (to borrow Kenneth Bailey's phrase).[121] In the West, we tend to think of hospitality as something we can choose to do or not do, depending on whether it is convenient for us. This is not so in the desert landscape and culture in which the Patriarchal accounts are set. Hospitality is to be extended not only to one's friends, but also to travellers, strangers and even enemies. This is one reason why Sisera could seek refuge in Jael's tent, and why her actions in killing Sisera are so problematic (Judg 4:17-22).

The ANE (Ancient Near East) conventions for hospitality have been well set out elsewhere.[122] The visitors lodged in Lot's house could expect, in that culture, good treatment and protection, rather than the abuse

---

120. J.A. Loader, *A Tale of Two Cities: Sodom and Gomorrah in the Old Testament, Early Jewish and Early Christian Traditions* (Kampen: J. H. Kok, 1990), 37.

121. K.E. Bailey, *Jesus Through Middle Eastern Eyes: Cultural Studies in the Gospels* (London: SPCK, 2008).

122. For example, W.W. Fields, *Sodom and Gomorrah: History and Motif in Biblical Narrative* (JSOTSup 231; Sheffield: Sheffield Academic Press, 1997), 56. W.J. Lyons, *Canon and Exegesis: Canonical Praxis and the Sodom Narrative* (JSOTSup 352; Sheffield: Sheffield Academic Press, 2002), 162 gives a similar list.

they were threatened with.[123] The kind of hospitality expected in that society is shown in Abraham's welcome of three "men" just before the story of Sodom (Gen 18:1-8). Lot has shown appropriate hospitality by offering lodging to the two messengers who arrived in the town square at night (Gen 19:1-3). He would undoubtedly have found it a breach of his duty to expose his guests to the calls of those who gathered outside his house. Some try to make much of the "excessive" show of hospitality by Lot, perhaps implying he knew that they were more than men. But the rising, bowing down to the ground and strong urging are not atypical but rather strong echoes of Abraham's hospitality in Genesis 18:1-8. It is only excessive by Western standards, not by those of the narrative setting.

Thus, the twin grounds of violence and breach of hospitality would be sufficient grounds for Lot to say "no" to the men of Sodom. But the real issue is whether these were the only grounds for his action, or whether there was something else about the action itself that caused Lot to label their proposal as wicked. While there was clearly inhospitality and abuse involved, Wenham argues that it was their sinful homosexual intentions which added "a special piquancy" to their offence.[124] Grenz argues that it does involve sexual acts, perhaps as a way in that culture of humiliating a defeated enemy by treating them as a woman.[125] They did not seek homosexual acts for the sake of sexual gratification, but as a way of humiliating and showing the subordinate status of these travellers. So Grenz argues that "the men of Sodom were guilty of twisting God's good intention for human sexuality into a vehicle for unjust treatment of visitors to their city."[126]

---

123. So T.M. Bolin, "The Role of Exchange in Ancient Mediterranean Religion and Its Implications for Reading Genesis 18-19," *JSOT* 29 (2004): 48. See also Lyons, *Canon and Exegesis*, 225-234.

124. G.J. Wenham, "The Old Testament Attitude to Homosexuality," *ExpTimes* 102 (1991): 359-363, 361.

125. Grenz, *Welcoming But Not Affirming*, 39.

126. Grenz, *Welcoming But Not Affirming*, 40.

Warner seems to assume that, because their proposed action would be wrong in terms of violence and breach of hospitality, then the issue of this being homosexual activity cannot be considered. This does not follow logically. A more reasonable view is that this action is (rightly) regarded by Lot as wicked on three grounds—it is a breach of hospitality; it is forced rather voluntary; and it involves a prohibited form of sexual activity i.e. homosexual intercourse. Thus, Grenz concludes that Derek Bailey and others have not been able to sustain the claim that the homosexual dimensions of the sin of Sodom are just incidental.[127]

Lust or Hubris?

A couple of minor issues need some clarification. The first is whether this would count as "homosexual" activity anyway, since it did not envisage sexual intercourse between the men of Sodom and other men, but rather between men and "heavenly" (better than "divine") beings or angels. However, we need to bear in mind that neither Lot nor the men of Sodom knew that the "messengers" (the essential meaning of "angels") were not human beings but heavenly beings. In v.5, the men of Sodom ask for "the men who came to you tonight"; in v.8, Lot pleads with the men of the town to "do nothing to these men."

The intended action and Lot's response that this is wickedness, are both assuming that it is sexual activity between men and other men. While it is true that, if the proposed activity took place, it would technically not have been homosexual activity, the moral evaluation in the story is based on the intended action which was clearly sexual intercourse between men and men.

This helps to clarify Warner's next possibility of whether this might instead be human *hubris* of trying to gain divinity through sexual relations with "divine beings." A number of responses can be made. Firstly, angels are "heavenly (as opposed to earthly) beings" not "divine beings." Secondly, the goal had nothing to do with *hubris* as the men were not aware of the identity of the messengers. Had

---

127.   Grenz, *Welcoming But Not Affirming* 40.

they been successful, it would certainly have been a crossing of a forbidden boundary (perhaps Genesis 6:1-4), but it was never intended as an assault with the aim of becoming "divine." Thirdly, it was not pride which motivated the men, but lust, either for sex or power or both.

Genesis 19 and Judges 19

Warner helpfully draws attention to the parallel account of Judges 19, and concedes that any angelic messengers (= her 'divine beings") do not appear there. Two comments are worth making. Firstly, Judges 19 is dependent on Genesis 19 rather than *vice versa*. Lasine describes this as a one-sided literary dependence since "a reader can fully understand the story of Lot's hospitality in Sodom without knowing the story of the Levite's concubine," but not the other way around.[128] A more significant parallel for understanding Genesis 19 is in fact the hospitality shown by Abraham in Genesis 18:1-8.[129]

Secondly, if these are parallel accounts, this would also suggest that identifying these messengers as non-humans in Genesis 19 was not crucial to the interpretation of that chapter. It is likely that the point of both stories is found elsewhere.

Does Warner Conclude More Than She Has Established?

Warner makes a number of disputable claims in the concluding three paragraphs of her article. Firstly, she asserts that Genesis 19 was not popularly understood to refer to homosexual activity until one or two centuries before Christ. However, this has not been established in her article.

Secondly, she concludes that, because some recent scholars have argued that the sin of Sodom may have been *hubris*, inhospitality

---

128. S. Lasine, "Guest and Host in Judges 19: Lot's Hospitality in an Inverted World," *JSOT* 29 (1984): 38.

129. Lasine, "Guest and Host," 53 notes that "in order to fully understand Gen. 19 one does need to know the closely related story of Abraham's hospitality in Gen. 18, and the character of Lot as exhibited in Gen. 13."

or the abuse of power, then it is not about homosexuality, and it cannot have a single clear message but rather a range of possible meanings. However, this does not follow logically. The presence of other options does not preclude homosexuality as the theme or a theme (in conjunction with some others). Clearly, both issues of inhospitality and the abuse of power are present within the story (I think that *hubris* is not), but so too, I would argue, is the issue of homosexuality as a crossing over the boundary of Genesis 2.

Thirdly, she claims that there are good grounds for questioning the traditional understanding that views Genesis 19 as having implications for contemporary debates about homosexuality. In particular, "this biblical story can quite properly be read as having nothing to do with homosexuality."[130] This is to conclude far more than she has established. To argue that a text may be partly about *hubris*, inhospitality, abuse of power, or even non-consensual homosexual activity (which is the essence of her argument) does not lead to the conclusion that it cannot have any implications for the discussion of homosexuality. Her view is again undermined by a failure to consider the effect of Genesis 2 as a crucial background for the way in which Genesis 19 should be read.

Looking Towards Today

Of course, even if homosexuality as such were not the issue in Genesis 19, it does not follow that God approves of homosexual behaviour. Yet there are compelling grounds to see that Genesis 19 provides a window into God's view of homosexual activity, especially when read alongside the other biblical texts. The traditional view is worth believing, not because it is traditional, but because it best accounts for the text and contexts of Genesis 19. However, this passage also draws attention to God's opposition to any form of sexual violence, homosexual or heterosexual, and we must not be silent on such matters either.[131]

---

130. Warner, "Sodomites," 9.

131. This salutary reminder is raised by Webb, "Homosexuality in Scripture," 78.

CHAPTER 3

The Culpability of Sexual Offence: Understanding Leviticus 18:22 and 20:13 in Context

KATY SMITH

You shall not lie with a male as with a woman; it is an abomination. (Lev 18:22 NRSV).

If a man lies with a male as with a woman, both of them have committed an abomination; they shall be put to death; their blood is upon them. (Lev 20:13 NRSV)

Introduction

The claim of Richard Treloar's reading of Leviticus 18:22 and 20:13 in *Five Uneasy Pieces* is that the prohibitions against homosexual acts are plain in their meaning, but are unpalatable in the 21st century Australian context.[132] The conclusion of his argument is a plea for Anglicans to resist the plain meaning of Leviticus 18:22 and 20:13 for today. This raises two issues at stake in the current debate about whether homosexual acts are permissible within God's purposes for the world. The first is the authority of the Bible and the second is the meaning of the biblical texts that teach about the ethics of homosexual acts. Intriguingly, even the strongest proponents of gay marriage argue that the meaning of Leviticus 18:22 and 20:13 is indisputable,[133] yet is this true? Treloar's reading of Leviticus 18:22 and 20:13 raises key issues about the interpretation of these two texts within the context of the whole book that are vitally significant for understanding how they apply to Christian believers in the 21st century. In response to Treloar's plea to resist the plain meaning of these texts, the task of this chapter is to bring clarity to how we can read and understand Leviticus 18 and 20 within its context as Christian Scripture today.

---

132. Richard Treloar, "On 'Not Putting New Wine into Old Wineskins,', or 'Taking the Bible Fully Seriously': An Anglican Reading of Leviticus 18:22 and 20:13," in *Five Uneasy Pieces: Essays on Scripture and Sexuality* (Adelaide: ATF, 2011), 13-30.

133. "This is an issue of biblical authority. Despite much well-intentioned theological fancy footwork to the contrary, it is difficult to see the Bible as expressing anything else but disapproval of homosexual activity" Diarmaid MacCulloch, *Reformation: Europe's House Divided 1490–1700* (London: Penguin, 2004), 705.

Understanding the Purpose of Leviticus within its Narrative Framework

The book of Leviticus claims more than any other book in the Old Testament to be God's spoken word for his covenant people.[134] The narrative beginning of the book, "And he called to Moses and the LORD said to him from the tent of meeting saying, 'say to my people Israel ...'" (1:1–2),[135] alerts us as readers to the wider narrative framework and it is suggested that we could read from Exodus 40:34–35 to Leviticus 1:1 without any disruption to the flow of the narrative.[136] This continuity from Exodus to Leviticus accentuates the redemptive context within which Leviticus emerges. Constantly throughout the book, Yahweh reminds his people about his redemptive work rescuing Israel from slavery in Egypt and transferring the nation into relationship with him as their covenant God (e.g. 11:45; 18:2; 22:33; 25:38, 42, 55; 26:13). It is upon this basis that Yahweh calls his people to be holy as he, their covenant God, is holy (11:44-45). Yahweh recalls his work of redemption in the exodus event to remind the Israelites that they were brought out of Egypt to live in the land of promise for the sole purpose of belonging exclusively to Yahweh (22:33; 25:38). The ultimate goal of their redemption from Egypt was not the fulfilment of the promise of land, but so that Yahweh can be their God. Therefore, a major purpose of the book of Leviticus within its narrative framework is to teach God's covenant people to be set apart for Yahweh as their covenant God on the basis that they are a redeemed people who belong to Yahweh alone.

As Yahweh calls out to Moses from the tent of meeting in Leviticus 1:1–2 so that Moses might mediate his words to Israel, the reader cannot help but recall God's stated purpose for the tent of meeting

---

134.   Walter C. Kaiser, "Leviticus," in *New Interpreters Bible* ed. L.E. Keck (Nashville, TN: Abingdon, 1994), 1: 987.

135.   My translation.

136.   Nobuyoshi Kiuchi, *Leviticus* (Apollos Old Testament Commentary; Leicester: IVP, 2007), 16.

in Exodus 29:43–46. The tent of meeting is where firstly Yahweh will meet with Moses (Exod 29:42) and secondly he will meet with the Israelites (Exod 29:43). Verse 45 then provides the theological basis for the tabernacle, which is so that "I [Yahweh] will dwell among the people of Israel and will be their God." This purpose for the tabernacle is restated in Leviticus 26 as part of the covenant blessings. Yahweh reiterates in v. 11 his goal of making his dwelling among the people. After which a new dimension of the promise emerges in v. 12 where Yahweh will walk among them, be their God, and they will be his people. Hartley observes a link between Yahweh's promise to walk among his people with Enoch, Noah, and Abram having walked with God, but there is a significant difference in Leviticus 26:12, in that God is the one who is walking among his people.[137] Another allusion is possible, which is to Yahweh walking in the Garden of Eden (Gen 3:8), which "suggests that 'I will walk among you' is the blessing the Lord bestowed upon the first humans in Eden."[138]

"You shall be Holy to me for I the LORD am Holy"

The goal of Leviticus is therefore a right relationship between Yahweh and his people, which displays God's purpose for his creation. It is to this end that the book of Leviticus teaches God's people how to be set apart for him as their covenant God. Treloar's understanding of the book's purpose diminishes its theological value especially in regards to Israel's holiness. First, Treloar states, "nearness to God is predicated on ritual purity and holiness."[139] Yet it is evident from our brief overview of the book's goal within its narrative framework

---

137. John E. Hartley, *Leviticus* (Word Biblical Commentary; Dallas, Texas: Word, 1992), 463.

138. Kiuchi, *Leviticus*, 478. "The choice of the Hitpa'el is theologically significant: God will walk with his people, as he walked with Adam and Eve in the Garden of Eden ... That is, God's blessings can bring a return of paradisiacal conditions" (Jacob Milgrom, *Leviticus 23–27* [AB; New York: Doubleday, 2001], 2302). See also Gordon J. Wenham, *The Book of Leviticus* (NICOT; Grand Rapids, MI: Eerdmans, 1979), 330.

139. Treloar, "Not Putting New Wine into Old Wineskins," 21.

that it is not "nearness to God" but rather the imminence of God to his people, which is made possible through God's provision of instruction about how to be a people set apart for him as their covenant God. Second, Israel's holiness, in Treloar's argument, is their separation by God from the other nations, and their response is to ritually "separate the sacred from the profane." He then states, "to this end (Israel's holiness as separateness) God does a lot of prohibiting in Leviticus."[140] However, it will be evident through a brief discussion of God's work of separation and of Israel's holiness that Treloar overemphasises Israel's separation *from the nations* rather than balancing this with Israel being separated *for Yahweh*.

Treloar refers to Leviticus 20 as the *a priori* of his argument where the verb "to separate" occurs four times with in vv. 24–26, which Milgrom suggests is arranged in a chiastic structure.[141] This chiastic structure outlined below aligns Yahweh having separated Israel from the nations in v. 24b and v. 26 with the separation between pure and impure animals that Israel was to make in v. 25.[142]

A (v. 24b)	I am the LORD your God I have *separated* you from the peoples
B (v. 25a)	You shall therefore make a *distinction*1 between the clean animal and the unclean, and between the bird and the clean;

---

140. Treloar, "Not Putting New Wine into Old Wineskins," 22.

141. Based on Jacob Milgrom, *Leviticus 17–22* (Anchor New York: Doubleday, 2000), 1761, although the NRSV translation has been substituted for Milgrom's translation of the Hebrew text. A chiastic structure is a diagonal or crisscross arrangement with reversed words in the second half of two parallel phrases.

142. Philip Peter Jenson, *Graded Holiness: A Key to the Priestly Conception of the World, Journal of the Society of Old Testament Studies* (JSOTSS 106; Sheffield: JSOT, 1992), 145.

B' (v. 25b)	You shall not bring abomination on yourselves by animal or by bird or by anything with which the ground teems, which I have *set apart* for you to hold unclean.
A' (v. 26)	You shall be holy to me; for I the LORD am holy, And I have *separated* you from the other peoples to be mine.

Significantly, v. 26 associates God's act of separating Israel from the nations with Yahweh's command to Israel to imitate his holiness. On this basis, Milgrom argues that Israel's holiness is both the imitation of God as well as separation from the nations. He rightly observes that the meaning of "to be holy" is to be set apart *for* something as well as being set apart *from* something.[143] In the case of Israel, they are to be set apart *from* the nations and *for* Yahweh their covenant God. Being set apart from the nations is not the end or the goal, but rather being set apart for Yahweh is the goal of their distinctiveness. The reason why God has set apart Israel from the nations is so that they can be solely for him.

Ritual or Ethical Purity?

Treloar's understanding of Israel's holiness as separation from the nations or differentiation is an unbalanced view of holiness that does not take into account being set apart *for* Yahweh. Our argument is that the goal of Israel's separation from the nations is for an exclusive allegiance to Yahweh their covenant God. Yahweh achieved this separation in their redemption, but in response Israel is to be distinct ethically from the nations and for their covenant God who is a holy God. This is contrary to Treloar's argument that the response Israel is to make to their separation from the nations is

---

143.   Milgrom, *Leviticus 17–22*, 1762.

to ritually separate the "sacred from the profane."[144] He emphasises Israel's holiness as a ritual distinctiveness which extends from the sanctuary (the emphasis in Leviticus 1–16) to "beyond the sanctuary to embrace the entire land" in Leviticus 17–26.[145] However, it is vitally important that we recognise that Israel's holiness in Leviticus 17–26 contains the idea of ethical distinction.[146] The distinction between the pure and impure animals and birds in 20:25 is a pedagogical exercise to learn about imitating God in setting apart the profane from the holy and being distinct,[147] but Israel's call to be holy from

---

144. Norman Snaith, *Leviticus and Numbers* (New Century Bible (NCB); London: Oliphants, 1969), 67, also attributes Israel's call to holiness in Leviticus 11:44–45 as ritual purity and then builds an argument for Leviticus 17–26 as being about religious rather than ethical conduct. His argument, though, is based on the notion that Israel is to follow these commands because they are the "will of their Saviour God" rather than that they are ethical (Snaith, *Leviticus*, 85). However, there is no distinction between God's purpose and what is ethical for the basis of biblical ethics is the imitation of God. Milgrom too makes this point, "Holiness means not only 'separation from' but 'separation to.' It is a positive concept, an inspiration and a goal associated with God's nature and his desire for man ... that which man is commanded to emulate and approximate, is what the Bible calls ... 'holy.' Holiness means *imitatio Dei*." (Jacob Milgrom, *Leviticus 1–16* [Anchor Bible; New York: Doubleday, 1991], 731).

145. Treloar, "Not Putting New Wine into Old Wineskins," 22–23. Treloar misquotes Milgrom's argument that is making the point that there is a relationship between the created order and God's work in separating Israel from the nations. Milgrom does not mention Treloar's point that Leviticus 17–26 is extending ritual purity from "the domain of the sacred beyond the sanctuary to embrace the entire land...' , nor is this inferred (Jacob Milgrom, *Leviticus: A Book of Ritual and Ethics (Continental; Minneapolis, MN: Fortress, 2004), 179).* While Leviticus 17-26 does expand the view of the holy from cultic elements in chapters 1–16 to encompass the whole people of Israel, this is not an expansion of ritual holiness but includes ethical holiness (Jacob Milgrom, "The Changing Concepts of Holiness in the Pentateuchal Codes with Emphasis on Leviticus 19," in *Reading Leviticus: A Conversation with Mary Douglas,* ed. John F. A. Sawyer [Sheffield: Sheffield Academic Press, 1996], 68–69).

146. Milgrom, *Leviticus 1–16, 730.* See also Hartley, *Leviticus,* lx.

147. "By regulating a myriad of daily matters, these laws on ritual purity sought to ingrain the concept of the holy into the social consciousness of the people ... By the daily observance of the ritual laws, a person sanctifies himself, developing a noble character that is in accord with the moral law"

the nations and to Yahweh their God is an ethical purity based in the imitation of God's holiness.[148]

The Book of Leviticus and Genesis 1–3

Treloar observes, albeit briefly, how the use of the verb "to separate" in the book of Leviticus alludes to the first creation story, but he does not relate the significance of this observation to the rest of his argument.[149] Indeed, the prominence of Yahweh's work of separation clustered in Leviticus 11 and 20 echoes his creative work of separation within Genesis 1:1–2:3 that encompasses distinguishing the light from the darkness (vv. 4, 18), separating the waters to distinguish from the waters above the dome to the waters underneath (vv. 6–7), and separating the day and the night (v. 14). The purpose of separation within God's handiwork is to provide order within creation as well as distinguishing between different parts so that each part of creation has its role. Overall, the act of separating and distinguishing between parts of creation accentuates God's role as the lawgiver and as a God of purpose and intentionality.

The allusions to God's creative work of separation for the purpose of distinction within the book of Leviticus are profound and impact our understanding of sexual offence both in Leviticus 18 and 20. When we read in Leviticus 20:24–26 the fourfold emphasis upon God's work of separation and distinction firstly within the domain of separating Israel from the nations and then within the domain of distinguishing the impure animals and birds from the pure, we witness once again God setting apart in order to bring distinction and order as the lawgiver. This is a purposeful connection for it relates God's work of separation in creation and his work of separation

---

(Hartley, *Leviticus*, lx).

148. For an argument that is the reversal of Treloar's view of ritual vs ethical holiness, see Leigh M. Trevaskis, *Holiness, Ethics and Ritual in Leviticus* (Hebrew Bible Monographs (HBM) 29; Sheffield: Sheffield Phoenix, 2011), which argues that an ethical dimension of Israel's holiness is not isolated to Leviticus 17–26 but is also present in Leviticus 1–16.

149. Treloar, "Not Putting New Wine into Old Wineskins," 21.

in redemption.[150] God's work of redemption in the exodus event, where he acted to separate Israel from all the nations of the earth so that they can belong to him, is a continuation of God's creative work where he intends to re–create right order in the world through his nation. In Leviticus 20, this right order that God is creating is ethical. Israel is to be set apart from the nations and to Yahweh for the purpose of restoring order that reflects God's creative purposes. This is his prerogative as the sovereign creator and lawgiver.

There is, however, another instance of separation and distinction in Genesis 1 that we have not yet mentioned. In Genesis 1:27, Yahweh as the lawgiver makes a distinction within humankind between male and female. First God accentuates their unity ("God created humankind") but then purposefully separates humankind into male and female ("male and female he created them"). This distinction in unity emerges again in the second creation story where woman is created from the man emphasising that they are made of the same matter while clearly maintaining the distinction between "woman" and "man" (2:23-24).[151] The distinction between man and woman is maintained in the context of a covenantal marriage relationship where the man leaves his father and mother to become "one flesh" with his wife.[152] Thus, the distinction between male and female is part of God's created order as is covenantal marriage that maintains the distinction within their unity. When we explore Leviticus 20, it will be evident that the order of sexual offence outlined in Leviticus 20:9–16 deviates from this principle of male–female covenant marriage relationship, which is part of God's created order, in increasing degrees of magnitude from this norm. The greater the

150.   Milgrom, *Leviticus 17–22*, 1761–1762.

151.   See also David Peterson, "Holiness and God's Creation Purpose" in *Holiness & Sexuality: Homosexuality in a Biblical Context* ed. David Peterson (Milton Keynes: Paternoster, 2004), 8.

152.   Gordon J. Wenham, *Genesis 1–15* (WBC; Waco, Texas: Word, 1987), 71, observes that the two verbs "forsake" and "cleave" in the "context of Israel's covenant with the LORD suggests that the OT viewed marriage as a kind of covenant."

degree of deviation, the greater the degree of disorder. When the degree of disorder reaches confusion, the sexual offence is called a perversion (in the case of bestiality) because it mixes where there is to be separation and distinction. Therefore, what Israel was commanded to do ritually (that is, separate the impure from the pure for the purpose of distinction) is mirrored in the ethical domain, except that while ritual impurity led to temporary exclusion from God's presence and the camp, the consequences of sexual offence are death or permanent exile.

Understanding Sexual Offence in Leviticus 18 and 20

Treloar states, "there seems to be little support for readings which cast these verses as anything other than prohibitive with respect to homosexual acts."[153] Later he observes that "illicit sexual unions" are understood to be a confusion of the creation boundaries. Disregarding this line of argument, he then focuses on the importance of ordered procreation in Israel's context in order to maintain their distinct identity among mightier nations.[154]

---

153.   Treloar, "Not Putting New Wine into Old Wineskins," 22.

154.   Treloar, "Not Putting New Wine into Old Wineskins," 25. Milgrom, *Leviticus 17-27* 1568, proposes this argument on the basis that a prohibition against female–female intercourse is absent with the conclusion "The legal reason for interdicting anal intercourse ... is the waste, the nonproductive spilling, of seed" and then proposes "if gay partners adopt children, they do not violate the intent of the prohibition." This intent, according to Milgrom, *Leviticus 17–27* 1568, is preserving "procreation within a stable family." While the context of Leviticus 18:22 suggests a major concern with right family relationships (see Jonathan Burnside, *God, Justice, and Society: Aspects of Law and Legality in the Bible* [New York: Oxford, 2011], 351–352), there are only two references to "seed" within Leviticus, which occur within the two verses directly preceding the prohibition against homosex in 18:22. In the first instance in v. 20, the command is against giving seed in sexual intercourse to a neighbour's wife. The second instance in v. 21 concerns not giving seed to sacrifice to Molech, which would profane Yahweh's name. The emphasis within these two verses is to whom the seed has been given rather than a shameful loss of seed. In the first occurrence, the giving of seed through sexual intercourse is in the context of adultery, while the second is in dedication to an idol. There is no concern here for orderly procreation but rather preserving right relationship between the neighbour and Yahweh. This is therefore more in keeping with the commands of the Decalogue rather than a social concern for procreation.

However, there is insufficient textual support for understanding this to be a major reason for the prohibition against homosexual acts. An analysis of the prohibitions within the context of each chapter reveals a different concern, which is for God's purpose of right order in sexual relationships. Any act that contravenes this right order is considered to be a sexual offence.

Understanding Sexual Offence in Leviticus 18

Leviticus 18 is well ordered structurally with three major sections. The first section in vv. 1–5 provides the motivation for obedience, which is their exclusive allegiance to Yahweh as their God and the promise of life. In contrast, the last section in vv. 24–30 uses language of curse and exile if God's people make themselves impure through the offences outlined within the central section (vv. 6–23). This central section has a different tone to vv. 1–5 and vv. 24–30. The prohibitions in vv. 6–23 are apodictic law that conveys principles of law and are therefore absolute. This type of law does not give the consequence of disobedience, but straightforwardly sets out what is not an acceptable standard of behaviour, which in this case, is for all who live in the land of promise whether they are an Israelite or a foreigner (v. 26). Verse 6 provides the beginning principle, "None of you shall approach anyone near of kin to uncover nakedness." This can also be rendered more literally as "No man is to come near a flesh of his flesh to uncover their nakedness: I am the LORD."[155] This general principle is then applied in vv7–18 to cases of relationships that descend in order of proximity, from the closest relative to the more distant relative.

Verses 19–23 then continue to address the issue of sexual offences with those who are unrelated to the man. The prohibitions in vv. 19–23 depart from the norm of a male–female covenantal marriage relationship in increasing degrees of magnitude. Verse 19 maintains the norm of a male–female relationship but the offence is a male sexual act with a woman who is menstruating and who is therefore impure. The first question that arises in our 21st century mindset is

---

155. My translation.

why this prohibition exists and the second question is why having sex with a menstruating woman is a deviation from the created norm. Leviticus 15:19-24 is clear that a menstruating woman is impure (v.9) and moreover, when a woman begins menstruating while having sex with a man, the man becomes impure for seven days as well (v. 24). Impurity within Leviticus 11–15 is associated with that which is symbolic of disorder. When blood is in its right place, that is, inside the body or used in sacrifice, then this is a sign of life, wholeness, and order. However, when the body loses blood, the blood is out of place and thus is a sign of unwholeness and disorder as well as symbolising death. Wenham observes the profound nature of the laws: "Anyone losing blood is at least in danger of becoming less than perfect and therefore unclean. Thus blood is at once the most effective ritual cleanser ("the blood makes atonement," 17:11) and the most polluting substance when it is in the wrong place."[156] Against this background, the prohibition against sex with a menstruating woman in 18:19 makes sense. The man knows that the woman is impure symbolising disorder and death and yet intentionally makes himself impure with her when she is off–limits. This is a wilful act that desires the state of impurity and disorder rather than a state of holiness and purity. It is a rejection of God and both his creative and redemptive purposes. For this reason, instruction that belonged in the ritual domain now has an ethical dimension. The reason why it is the first deviation from the norm is because the prohibition is within a male–female covenant marriage relationship while the next prohibition in v. 20 is with a neighbour's wife, and deviates one more degree from the norm of a male–female marriage relationship.[157]

The next two deviations in vv. 22–23 represent the complete departure from the male–female marriage relationship. In v. 22, the divergence is a male taking the place of a female in an act of male–male sexual intercourse and for the first time in the

---

156. Wenham, *Leviticus* 186.

157. The NRSV translates "neighbour" as "kinsman" but the meaning of the Hebrew in this instance is of another man who is not connected by flesh and blood.

chapter the sexual offence in question is called an "abomination."[158] Treloar argues that "abomination" has primarily a cultic meaning due to the use of the word in other contexts. However, we must be careful about importing meaning into a word from how that particular word is used in other contexts. It is wise to preserve the meaning of the word's lexical root, which in this case is "to abhor" or "to detest".[159] The primary meaning in 18:22 and 20:13 is that this particular offence, which is homosexual activity, is detestable to God and by implication should be detestable to his people.[160] The last sexual offence that completely deviates from the male–female covenantal marriage norm is when either a man or a woman has sexual intercourse with an animal. The complete departure from God's purpose for his creation and into bestiality is evident by the calling of the human–animal sexual act a "perversion", which in the Hebrew means "confusion". In this instance, it is a confusion of the distinction between humanity and animals. It is noticeable that the command against offering children (literally "seed") as a sacrifice to Molech in v. 21 interrupts the order of sexual offences. However, this disruption is quite purposeful because the law in v. 21 separates the laws about male–female sexual offences from vv. 22–23, which contain deviations from the male–female relationship.

The prohibition against homosexual acts is therefore within a wider context of sexual offences. The seriousness of all sexual offences within Leviticus 18 is heightened with the warring of covenant curses in vv. 24–30 for disobedience. Verse 24 is clear that committing a sexual offence will defile the people and the land. It is not simply a case of impurity, but the complete reversal of their holiness. The consequence will be that the offenders will bear the same penalty as the nations previously inhabiting the land. There is no substitute and no mitigation of the penalty. Treloar argues that the kind of impurity referred to within the Holiness Code (Lev 17–27) is a ritual

---

158. See also Peterson, "Holiness and God's Creation Purpose," 7.

159. Wenham, *Leviticus,* 259.

160. Peterson, "Holiness and God's Creation Purpose," 7.

impurity. However there is always a way to atone through ritual for ritual impurity, whereas there is no such provision for impurity in Leviticus 18.[161] The defilement of a sexual offence is irreversible by ritual. The only way to atone for the defilement caused by sexual offences is by being cut off from God, his people, and the land (vv. 28–29). God's purpose for the land of promise is for God's people to model right relationship with him, one another, and with the land. Verses 28–30 indicate that a sexual offence defiles each of these three dimensions of relationship and is therefore contrary to not only God's creative purposes but also his redemptive purposes as well.

Understanding the Penalty for Sexual Offence in Leviticus 20

While Leviticus 18 uses apodictic law to express the absolute nature of sexual offence, Leviticus 20 in contrast is casuistic law that states what must be done in a specific situation. Casuistic law is outcome–oriented, which acts to accentuate the penalty for offence in Leviticus 20. Again, the structure of the chapter is well ordered and helps us to understand the passage as a whole.[162] First, Leviticus 20 employs parallelism as a double "book–end" (or *inclusio*) to the chapter:[163]

A   Ban on Molech worship and necromancy (vv. 1–6)

B   Call to holiness and obedience to God's instructions (vv. 7–8)

B'   Call to holiness and obedience to God's instructions (vv. 22–26)

A'   Ban on Molech worship and necromancy (v. 27)

The use of parallelism to encompass the whole chapter stresses the ban on idolatry and the practices tied up with idolatry especially

---

161.   Milgrom, *Leviticus 17–22,* 1573.

162.   Contrary to Hartley, *Leviticus* 331, who states, "Based on subject matter, these laws seem to be randomly ordered", although their unity is based on shared key terms.

163.   Kiuchi, *Leviticus,* 368.

when those practices involve the dead. Equally the inner *inclusio* focuses the hearers' attention on the command to imitate Yahweh's holiness, as he is their covenant God. Furthermore, the double *inclusio* draws the reader's attention to the central section in vv. 9–21.

Second, Leviticus 20 conveys the penalties for a series of offences encompassing Molech worship (vv. 2–5), necromancy (v. 6), cursing of parents (v. 9), and sexual offences (vv. 2–21). There are two parties that are responsible for undertaking the punishment of the offender(s), either God or the covenant people, and who actually executes the penalty depends on the type of punishment. If the penalty is exile (that is, being cut off from God and his people) then the executor of the penalty is Yahweh himself; if the penalty is death, then the people are responsible for the execution. The chapter alternates in its structure between humanity and God being responsible for the punishment of the offender(s):[164]

A   Humanity (v. 2)
B   God (vv. 3–6)
C   Humanity (vv. 9–16)
B'   God (vv. 17–21)
A'   Humanity (v. 27)

Structurally, this chiastic arrangement of the chapter draws our attention to vv. 9–16 as the focus. Verse 9 surprisingly is about what happens when someone curses their mother or father. The reason why they bear the blood of that parent is because when someone is cursed it is not merely a rejection of their authority, but desiring their destruction. Therefore, the offender must bear the blood of their parent, which is the penalty for murder. Then in v. 10, the list of offences and their penalties change their focus to sexual offences. Again, similarly to Leviticus 18, there is an order to the sexual offences listed. However, this time the first sexual offence is the first variation from the norm of sexual intercourse within a male–female covenantal marriage relationship where the sexual act is

---

164.   An abbreviated version from Burnside, *God, Justice, and Society*, 356.

between a man and a woman who is married to another man. From this point, the order departs in greater degrees away from God's created purpose for man and woman in a male–female covenantal marriage relationship. Burnside explains this departure from the norm in the following way:[165]

v. 10	Opposed to the narrative type of normal sexual relations because it concerns relations between one man and one woman who is already married to another man.
v. 11	Further opposed to the paradigm because the woman in question is *a family member,* as opposed to the wife of a neighbour.
v. 12	Offers a further variation on the "same family" by going to the next generation (daughter–in–law).
v. 13	Even further opposed because it is no longer one man and one woman but one man and another man.
v. 14	Further opposed than v. 13 because it is no longer one man and a sexual partner but one and two sexual partners. The mother and daughter are coming into contact through the same man.
v. 15	Still further opposed because it concerns relations between a man and an animal.
v. 16	Even further opposed than v. 15 is that the woman takes the initiative, and the male (animal) submits. In v. 15, the man has sexual relations with a beast, but he still behaves like a man, while in v. 16, the woman approaches the beast and behaves like a man. She performs the role of a man, but she also becomes like the beast by being the submissive partner. This is the most extreme case of confusion imaginable – so much so that it is impossible to tell apart the woman and the beast.

---

165.   Adapted from Burnside, *God, Justice, and Society* 363.

The reason for the changed order of sexual offences in Leviticus 20 in comparison to Leviticus 18 is to emphasise that any sexual activity outside of God's created purpose for a male–female covenant marriage relationship is impermissible for the covenant people of God. Leviticus 20 makes explicit what is implicit in Leviticus 18, which is that any alternative to a sexual relationship (committed or casual) to the male–female covenant marriage relationship is exactly that, an alternative to God's created order and purpose, and therefore expresses the desire of the offenders for their own rule rather than the wisdom of God.

An exploration of the penalties within Leviticus reveals three main types of execution formulas. The first is "shall be put to death" (vv. 2, 9–13, 15). The second is "I will set my face against them, and will cut them off from the people" (vv. 3–6, 17–18). The third formula is "shall bear their guilt" (vv. 18–19). Only the second formula is used within vv. 9–16 and even then there are two variations of the formula. The first is in v. 14 when the two women, albeit mother and daughter, come into contact with one another sexually through the man. The variation of the execution formula is that all three offenders are to be burned with fire. The second variation is in v. 16 where the woman and the animal are to be killed. Putting to death is a public exhibition while the penalty of being killed is an immediate action. The more severe penalties when a woman puts herself in the position of a man or becomes like a beast in the sexual acts are intentional. One of Treloar's observations is an absence of a prohibition against female–female sexual intercourse,[166] but as the saying goes "absence of evidence is not evidence of absence." In fact, the confusion of v. 16 (as well as the implicit contact of the two females in v. 14) implicitly includes female–female sexual acts and there is no need to include another sexual offence to the list. Furthermore, we must note that all the executions are absolutes. There is no means for atonement. This is a horrifying reality in the book of Leviticus. Chapters 1–7 carefully set out God's provision for

---

166.   Treloar, "Not Putting New Wine into Old Wineskins," 25. So also Milgrom, *Leviticus 17–26*, 1568.

the Israelites to maintain their covenant fellowship with God through a series of offerings and sacrifices for different purposes including burnt and guilt offerings for atonement of sin. Atonement involves the "delivery of a guilty party from punishment", the condition of the offended party to accept the penalty, the lessening of the penalty, and the appeasement of the offended.[167] The means provided within Leviticus 1–7 (and also Leviticus 16) is through an animal substitution so that the guilty may be delivered through the transfer of the penalty to the substitution so that mitigation can occur. In stark contrast, Leviticus 20, as with chapter 18, provides no means for substitution or mitigation by ritual to regain fellowship or peace with their covenant God. The only atonement available for sexual offence is the finality of death.

The Theological Perspective of Leviticus 18 and 20 Concerning Sexual Offence

Our exploration of Leviticus 18 and 20 within the context of the purpose of the book as a whole reveals a theological complexity that at its core is a central message about God and his creation purposes for his world. God's work of redemption set his people apart from the nations to be a holy people for himself as their covenant God. The goal of their redemption is for Yahweh to dwell in the midst of his people and be their God, and in doing so, God aims to actively restore his created order. The response of a grateful nation is to desire life with God in their midst through obedience and by imitating his holiness. The call for Israel to be holy is to maintain the separation from the nations in order to be distinct for Yahweh. This distinction has an ethical dimension of right living in accordance with God's created order. Arising from this context is the principle of sexual offence, which is any alternative for sex other than within God's purpose for a male–female covenantal marriage relationship. God's purpose for his creation is to maintain the distinction between male and female within their unity and this distinction is to be

---

167. Jay Sklar, *Sin, Impurity, Sacrifice, Atonement: The Priestly Conception* (HBM 2; Sheffield: Sheffield Phoenix, 2005), 60.

reflected in the covenant marriage relationship where the husband and wife become one flesh. Any deviation from this norm set by God as lawgiver within his creation is a sexual offence and thus, every sexual offence is culpable before the living God. In the case of homosexual acts, the penalty is death because it deviates so far from God's created order that there is no longer distinction and thus it brings disorder and impurity. Moreover, there is no provision for a substitutionary sacrifice or for mitigation of the penalty. Atonement is through the death of the offenders, which creates a permanent separation between God and the offenders, the offenders and the covenant people, and the offender and the land.

Looking Forward into the New Testament

The Apostle Paul in his letter to the Romans affirms the teaching about sexual offence from Leviticus 18:22 and 20:13. In vv. 26–27, Paul depicts both women and men exchanging natural relations for those that are "contrary to nature". In other words, male–male sexual acts and female–female sexual acts are contrary to God's created order and his purpose for humanity. Then in v. 32, Paul highlights the culpability of all who partake in the offences of vv. 29–30 because they knew that they deserved to die. More shocking is that those who approve of the offences outlined in vv. 29–30 are equally culpable. However, Romans 2–3 presents the greatest leveller, which is that no one has an excuse because the moment we pass judgment we stand condemned. Paul is clear that there is no distinction between the Jew and the Gentile for "all have sinned and fall short of the glory of God" (Rom 3:23) However, where there was no means of atonement provided other than taking the life of the offender(s) in Leviticus 20, God has provided a sacrifice of atonement that is substitutionary through Jesus taking the death we deserved and the full extent of God's anger against sin. Just as there is no distinction between Jew and Gentile because all have sinned, so too there is no distinction between those who have been justified by Christ Jesus (Rom 3:23-24). It is clear however that this justification is conditional upon faith in Jesus and those who do not believe still stand condemned before the living God.

For those who are justified by faith in Jesus, Paul is clear in Romans 6:1-14 that we are no longer to let sin reign in our bodies and obey its passions because Christ Jesus has set us free from the penalty of death. Not persisting in sexual offence (as with all other kinds of offence) is a grateful although costly response to the One who bore the greatest cost of all. Jesus says to those who seek life in him that they must take up their cross and follow him (Mk 8:34-35), which means that we are called to a costly way of living as a distinctive people set apart while being sent to continue God's mission in his world.

The call to imitate God's holiness is a theological principle that continues into the new covenant (1 Pet 1:15), but with the unfolding of God's plan in Christ, there is one significant difference. No longer are God's people to be set apart from the nations in a land for Yahweh their God, but Jesus' disciples are now sent into the world and yet are still to be distinctive. The work of sanctification (that is, the action of setting apart) is both the work of God in our redemption and also our responsibility as we offer our bodies as a living sacrifice, holy and acceptable to God (Rom 12:1). Paul expresses this point another way when he exhorts the Galatians to live by the Spirit and not by the desires of the flesh (Gal 5:16) because those who belong to Christ "have crucified the flesh with its passions and desires" (Gal 5:24). Thus, our call to be holy still has an ethical dimension, which Peter identifies when he calls God's people to be holy in conduct (1 Pet 1:16). The reason Peter gives for the imperative of holy conduct is the principle of the imitation of God found in Leviticus 11:44.

A Short Excursus: The Relevance of Leviticus 18:19 under the New Covenant

An objection to this argument could be to ask why the principles of sexual offence apply in the new covenant and yet not Leviticus 18:19 (included in the category of sexual offence) that refers to sex with a menstruating woman. The above explanation of 18:19 reveals that a significant theological principle that underpins the prohibition, which is that wilful sexual acts that purposefully rebel against God's created and redemptive purposes create disorder in relationship between the offender(s) and God. We noted that this prohibition takes the instruction from the ritual domain in Leviticus 15:19–24 and introduces an ethical dimension based on rebellion against Yahweh. As we move forward into the New Testament, the ritual dimension of purity laws from Leviticus 15 are fulfilled in Jesus in two ways. First, before his death, Jesus' actions demonstrate a priority of approaching unclean people such as the woman who had been bleeding for twelve years and those with leprosy, and he does this because of their faith. The statement to the woman who had been bleeding for twelve years in 5:34 indicates that the woman's faith has made her whole and that Jesus makes her whole through healing.

Second, in Jesus' death, blood is no longer a cause of disorder symbolising death but becomes the most powerful purifier in his atoning work and is a means of life (Rom 3:25; Heb 9:11–14, 22). Therefore, displaced blood is no longer considered impure. This however does not mean it is irrelevant because understanding how the law is fulfilled in Christ helps us to see the fullness of what Jesus has accomplished in his atoning sacrifice. However, while Jesus indicates that ritual purity instructions are fulfilled in him, he also teaches that the ethical dimension of the laws are still valid and relevant.[168] For instance, when the Pharisees noted that the disciples were eating with defiled hands in Mark 7:1–2, they accused Jesus of disregarding the law of Leviticus 15:11. Jesus appealed to the ethical teaching of the law in Mark 7:20–21 stating, "It is what comes out of a person that defiles. For it is from within, from the human heart, that evil intentions come..." Therefore, while Leviticus 15 and 18:20 is fulfilled in Christ, the ethical dimension still remains valid for people under the new covenant today, and even more so in response to Jesus' costly sacrifice of atonement. Any sexual act that wilfully rebels against God's creative and redemptive purposes is deserving of relational exile. While Jesus has died for us and purified us from our impurity and infirmity, we still must not deliberately take part in a sexual act that will cause offence to God, for when we do, we are

---

168. Wenham, *Leviticus,* 225.

saying that we desire our own purposes rather than the purposes of our Lord.

Contextualising Leviticus 18 and 20 in our 21st Century Context

Treloar argues that the application of Leviticus 18 and 20 today is intolerable and should be resisted. His argument depends upon the understanding of "holiness as differentiation" where Israel is to be different through separation from the nations. He sees this as flawed "in a world teeming with displaced persons" and in a country with a history of mistreatment of indigenous persons.[169] However, holiness is separation for the goal of distinction and under the new covenant our separation from the nations is fulfilled in Jesus so that we, as believers in Christ, can be sent into the world. What does not change from the old to the new is our call to be distinctive ethically. Leviticus 18 and 20 teaches us the seriousness of sexual offence before the living God because it disrupts his created order and brings disorder. This seriousness is heightened with the knowledge that homosexual acts are deserving of the penalty of death, but at the same time, the seriousness of sexual offence allows us to know how God's grace in Christ abounds because while we were still sinners, Christ took this penalty for us. Denying the seriousness of offence in Leviticus 18 and 20 is a denial of the gospel because it diminishes the work of Christ. Rather than encouraging people to resist the plain sense of Scripture, the best thing we can do for our world is to proclaim Christ crucified and risen for it is the only way that God has provided for those who are dead before him to be made alive and have peace with him in Christ. Leviticus 18 and 20 should not lead us to condemn, but motivate us to repentance and belief in Jesus through whom God is bringing his purpose for creation to its end, which is a redeemed creation with God dwelling in the midst of his people (Rev 21:3–4).

---

169. Treloar, "Not Putting New Wine into Old Wineskins," 27.

CHAPTER 4

Paul's Jewish View of Sexuality in Romans 1:26-27

MICHAEL BIRD AND SARAH HARRIS

For this reason God gave them up to degrading passions. Their women exchanged natural intercourse for unnatural, and in the same way also the men, giving up natural intercourse with women, were consumed with passion for one another. Men committed shameless acts with men and received in their own persons the due penalty for their error. (Rom 1:26-27 NRSV)

Introduction

The interpretation of Romans 1:26-27 has become a storm centre of exegetical debate about sexuality since Paul appears to very clearly reject both homosexual and lesbian sex as incompatible with God's purposes for human sexuality. In many mainline churches, especially among Anglicans, this has led to an energetic quest to reconcile the biblical injunctions against homosexuality that we find in Romans 1 with the prevailing cultural trend of affirming homosexual relationships in western societies. On the one hand, a traditionalist Anglican scholar like N.T. Wright can say that for Paul in Romans 1:26-27 "homosexual behaviour is a distortion of the creator's design and that such practices are evidence, not of the intention of any specific individual to indulge in such practice for its own sake, but of the tendency within an entire society for humanness to fracture when gods other than the true one are being worshipped."[170] Another Anglican scholar, A. Katherine Grieb provides a different perspective on the same text. Grieb admits that it is clear that Paul thought that same-sex relations were immoral. Nonetheless, she maintains "the fact that Paul has strong opinions about what is natural and unnatural does not necessarily mean that he is correct." Grieb claims that there can be "honest differences of opinion about what is natural in God's created order and therefore what reflects and gives glory to God."[171] Peta Sherlock's contribution in *Five Uneasy Pieces* on "Reading Romans as Anglicans" follows in much the same vein as Grieb and others, that there are legitimate

---

170.   N.T. Wright, "Romans," in *New Interpreter's Bible* ed. L.E. Keck (12 vols.; Nashville: Abingdon, 2002), 10.434.

171.   A. Katherine Grieb, *The Story of Romans: A Narrative Defense of God's Righteousness* (Louisville: Westminster John Knox, 2002), 30.

grounds for either reinterpreting or rejecting Paul's statements in Romans 1:26-27 that censure homosexual behaviour.[172] In light of this debate, and with respect to the recent efforts of some Australian Anglican leaders to popularise the approach to sexuality and Scripture found in *Five Uneasy Pieces*, the aim of this chapter is to set out what Paul says about homosexuality in Romans 1:26-27, to engage Sherlock's arguments at the textual level, and to make some suggestion as to how we as Christians and Anglicans should navigate our way around this complex subject.

Paul and Homosexuality in Romans

In Romans 1:24-32, Paul catalogues several impure and shameful behaviours that result from a rejection of God. In a nutshell, immorality follows on from idolatry as a concerted rejection of the one God leads to sinful behaviour. More specifically, in Romans 1:26-27, Paul focuses on the shame accruing in sexual immorality. When people "exchange" the glory of God for inglorious created things (1:23), and "exchange" the truth of God for a lie (1:25), then inevitably they also "exchange" the natural role of sex for the unnatural (1:27). The quintessential example of "dishonourable passions" is women and men doing what is sexually unnatural with each other and committing shameful sexual acts. In the case of men, the consequences of their deeds, the physical consequences associated with homoerotic acts, is the due reward that they receive for their immoral conduct.

Let us note that Paul's central claim is not to prove the inherent evil of homosexual acts, this is just assumed by his Jewish context; rather, his aim is to explain how such behaviour is an expression of divine wrath.[173] God punishes humanity for dishonouring him by allowing them to dishonour their very own bodies. Hence God deliberately "gives them over" (*paradidōmi*) to the over-powering of their desires (1:24, 26). In this giving-over, the restraints on dishonourable desires

---

172.   Peta Sherlock, "Reading Romans as Anglicans—Romans 1:26-27," in *Five Uneasy Pieces* (Adelaide: ATF, 2011), 31-45.

173.   Robert Jewett, *Romans* (Hermeneia; Minneapolis: Fortress, 2007), 173.

and the inhibitions towards degrading and impure acts are simply removed. Along this line Ernst Käsemann correctly observed that for Paul sexual perversion is "the result of God's wrath, not the reason for it."[174]

In the ancient world, one can find mixed things said about homosexual sex and same-sex relationships. In the Graeco-Roman world, generally speaking, same-sex relationships between women were routinely condemned, while homosexual acts by men were tolerable, though it was thought shameful for a man to allow himself to be the passive or penetrated partner in the sexual act.[175] Still, other Greek and Roman authors regarded homosexual acts with disdain. Juvenal mocked the drunken debauchery of women that often led to lesbian sexual acts.[176] The Socratic tradition of both Plato and Xenophon condemned homosexual acts.[177] The Old Testament resoundingly rejects homosexual practice (Lev 18:22; 20:13) and the rejection is continued in post-biblical Jewish literature as well.[178] For instance, the author of the *Epistle of Aristeas* typifies Jewish attitudes to pagan sexuality when he states that: "For they not only have intercourse with men but they defile their own mothers and even their daughters."[179] In *Sibylline Oracles* the author condemns the Phoenicians, Egyptians, and Latins who "hold unholy intercourse with boys."[180]

---

174. Ernst Käsemann, *Commentary on Romans* (trans. G.W. Bromiley; Grand Rapids, MI: Eerdmans, 1980), 47.

175. Cf. survey of literary evidence in Thomas K. Hubbard, *Homosexuality in Greece and Rome: A Sourcebook of Basic Documents* (Berkeley, CA: University of California Press, 2003).

176. Juvenal, *Satire* 6.306-13.

177. Plato, *Symposium* 217-19; Xenophon, *Memorabilia* 2.1.32.

178. Cf. Philo, *Abraham* 135-36; *Special Laws* 2.50; *T.Levi* 14.6; 17.11; *T.Naph.* 4.1; *2 Enoch* 10.4; *Sib. Or.* 3.185-87, 594-600, 763; 5.386-433; Josephus, *Against Apion* 2.25, 199.

179. *Ep. Arist.* 152.

180. *Sib. Or.* 3.596-97.

We think that Paul's remarks here, however out of step they are with contemporary views of sexual freedom, would be perceived as good news. First, if many of the Gentile Christians in Rome were slaves, then they were open to frequent sexual abuse and exploitation by their masters. Young boys were often captured, imported, sold, and then prostituted into sexual slavery. Paul's remarks represent an entrée into the plight of present and former slaves who resented sexual exploitation of themselves and their children in a culture typified by an aggressive bisexuality.[181] Second, for those Christians who were slave owners, who might have previously participated in symposia (drinking parties) with homoerotic pleasures, used male prostitutes, or engaged in homosexual relationships, they could see their former way of life as an experience of divine wrath, a wrath that they have now escaped from by coming under the Lordship of Jesus Christ.

Central to Paul's critique of female and male homosexuality is its unnaturalness as indicated by his use of the word *phusikos* for "nature/natural." Paul's phrase *para physin* is best translated as "contrary to nature" since the natural use of sex organs is exchanged for something else. He says that women exchanged "the natural use [of men] for what is contrary to nature [i.e. lesbianism]" and that men left the "natural use of women [i.e. in the sexual act]" and instead become inflamed with lust for one another. As Robert Gagnon points out, Paul, minimally, is referring to the anatomical and procreative complementarity of men and women as their sexual organs are designed for each other, something not true of gay sex.[182]

Paul was not alone in this judgment of the unnaturalness of homosexuality as such views were widespread in Greek, Roman, and Jewish literature. Plato spoke of sexual relations between men and between women as "contrary to nature."[183] Diodorus Siculus

---

181.   Jewett, *Romans,* 180-81.

182.   Robert A. J. Gagnon, *The Bible and Homosexual Practice: Texts and Hermeneutics* (Nashville: Abingdon, 2001), 254.

183.   Plato, *Laws* 1.2 (636 B.C.).

called homoerotic relationships "a marriage against nature".[184] Ovid had a girl involved in a same-sex relationship say "nature does not will it."[185] Pseudo–Lucian wrote about "a sacred law of necessity that each should retain its own nature and that neither should the female grow unnaturally masculine nor the male be unbecomingly soft."[186] Josephus rhetorically asked, "Why do not the Eleans and Thebans unleash that unnatural desire, which makes men engage in sexual intercourse?" and he argued that the sexual habits of Greek gods were simply a mythic story used to justify "unnatural pleasures."[187] In the ethically rigorous *2 Enoch* we read: "This place [i.e. hell], O Enoch, is prepared for those who dishonour God, who on earth practice sin against nature, which is child-corruption after the sodomitic fashion."[188] Philo says of the men of Sodom that not only did they engage in adultery, but "men mounted men, suffering defilement, and not respecting nature." As a result God, in his mercy, increased "the natural desire of men and women for a union together, for the sake of producing children, and detesting the unnatural and unlawful deeds of the people of Sodom."[189] In the Testament of the Twelve Patriarchs, the audience is exhorted not to be like the people of Sodom who, when it came to sex, "exchanged the order of its nature."[190] Finally, in Pseudo-Phocylides, roughly contemporary with Paul, one reads the injunction: "Do not transgress with unlawful sex the limits set by nature. For even animals are not pleased by intercourse of male with male. And let women not imitate the sexual role of men."[191] The same perspective continued into the

---

184.   Diodorus Siculus, *Hist*. 32.10.9.3.

185.   Ovid, *Metamorphoses* 9.758.

186.   Ps.-Lucian, *Erotes* 19.

187.   Josephus, *Apion* 2.273-75 (own trans.).

188.   *2 Enoch* 10.4.

189.   Philo, *Abraham* 135, 137 (own trans.).

190.   *T.Naph*. 3.4

191.   Ps.-Phocylides, *Sentences,* 190-93.

early church.[192] John Chrysostom, commenting on Romans 1:26-27, says that perpetrators of homosexual acts "dishonoured that which was natural, they ran after that which was contrary to nature," and he does not mince his words when he avers the reason why, "their doctrine [was] Satanical, and their life too was diabolical."[193]

The appeal to nature in this literature requires some earnest reflection. The realm and experience that is called "nature" is not a neutral sphere. What is regarded as "nature" and "natural" is very much constructed on the basis of a particular cultural framework. For instance, those of us with access to the Discovery Channel may think of "nature" as a thing of wonder and beauty to behold. Yet for those who are forced to eke out a pre-industrial living in the Amazonian rainforest, they may regard "nature" as an enemy of one's mortal existence and something that is savage as it is inescapable. In Stoic philosophy the natural world is divine, so that *natura* was a virtual god, known by common instinct, and ingrained within the very fabric of one's own being. For the Stoics, natural law directs people to select what is natural and to reject what is contrary to nature. Virtue consists of acting in accordance with the law of nature. Moreover, people have tried to argue that all sorts of things are authoritative, normative, and true because they accord with nature, ranging from Capitalism to Marxism, from egalitarianism to patriarchy. In fact, the argument against homosexual practices from nature can be turned on its head. Many today will argue that homosexuality is natural because it is programmed into people's genetic make-up and that gay dolphins and gay penguins somehow legitimate homosexual behaviour for *homosapiens*. In all of these appeals to nature we must be cognisant of the fact that "nature" is a culturally constructed; not a self-evident and universal norm known immediately to all. What is more, we should also heed various logical fallacies in applying nature to ethics. First, the naturalistic fallacy in that it is logically

---

192. Cf. Polycarp, *Phil. 5.3*; Aristides, *Apology* 17; *Acts of Thomas* 6.55; Tertullian, *Resurrection of the Flesh* 16.6; Clement of Alexandria, *Paedogogus* 2.10.83.3; 3.3.21.3.

193. John Chrysostom, *Hom. Rom.*

impossible to derive an "ought" from an "is", so that the gayness or straightness of dolphins proves only that dolphins have certain sexual habits; it does not thereby legitimate human gayness or straightness. Second, the naturalistic fallacy entails that the qualities of "right" and "wrong" are themselves non-natural entities and are derived from other beliefs, and not deduced from observing empirical phenomena. In other words, it is impossible to derive an ethical prescription from a mere description of natural processes.

That caveat about nature aside, we have to remember that for Paul and for Jewish thought more broadly, "nature" stands for the created order of things designed and put into effect by God and showcases God's very own glory.[194] For Paul, "nature" is divine architecture and doxological theatre. If we take Romans 1:26-28, 1 Corinthians 7:1-40, 11:1-16 together, then it is clear that sexuality is intrinsic to human bodily existence and that heterosexuality in particular was part of the divinely created order for humanity. Departures from the norm of God's creation represent defiance against the Creator and foreshadow the divine wrath soon to follow. To suppress the truth about the one God who made the heavens and the earth invariably leads to a rejection of God's design for sex as a means of partnership and procreation between men and women. Paul's appeal to nature is not based on the pantheism and natural law theory of Stoic philosophy, but rests squarely in his creational monotheism. Richard Hays puts it well: "The understanding of 'nature' in this conventional language does not rest on an empirical observation of what actually exists; instead, it appeals to an intuitive conception of what ought to be, of the world as designed by God. Those who indulge in sexual practices *para physin* are defying the creator and demonstrating their own alienation from him."[195]

Also important to note is that neither is Paul dealing with pederasty, even though it formed a large part of homosexual practice in the

---

194. Cf. discussion in Samuel H. Dresner, "Homosexuality and the Order of Creation," *Judaism* 40 (1991): 309-21.

195. Richard B. Hays, *The Moral Vision of the New Testament: Community, Cross, New Creation* (New York: Harper One, 1996), 194.

ancient Mediterranean world.[196] Greek society even more so than Roman society, accepted a variegated pattern of sexual behaviour ranging from the use of male and female slaves as sexual "partners," through to pederasty, the sexual exploitation of young boys. Paul's specification of lesbianism alongside homosexuality in Romans 1:26-27 makes explicit that he is addressing same-sex practice and not pederasty or any variant form.[197] What is helpful to note is that Paul makes a strongly egalitarian claim that both male and female same-sex relationships are judged equally even though Graeco-Roman society deemed the lesbian relationship as *para physin* while the homosexual relationship had some social acceptance. For Paul, both males and females were equally at risk of idolatry and, as we read on in Paul's letter, equally able to be set free by the Spirit (Rom 8:1-4).

Response to Peta Sherlock's Uneasy Piece

In light of the foregoing exegesis we can now make an informed evaluation of Peta Sherlock's argument for the inclusion of gay and lesbian relationships in the Anglican Church.

First, we acknowledge and approve of her hermeneutical approach of reading the whole of Scripture and reading Scripture eschatologically when it comes to the biblical witness on sexuality. But we feel that such moves will not provide the biblical warrant that she so desperately craves for same-sex relationships. That is because Scripture speaks unanimously against same-sex acts and Christ's return will involve a renewal of creation to its perfect and pre-fall state where men and women will dwell together in the new creation as co-image bearers and co-stewards of God's new creation (i.e. *Endzeit* will be as the *Urzeit—end time will be as primeval or original time*). Since homosexuality is a departure from God's purpose for creation and humanity it will have no place in the new creation. Indeed, as Jesus points to with the Sadducees

---

196.   Craig S. Keener, *Romans* (NCCS; Eugene, OR: Cascade, 2009), 37.

197.   This is widely agreed see Jewett, *Romans* 177; Keener, *Romans*, 39.

over the woman with seven husbands, eschatologically sex and marriage for heterosexuals will also take a cosmic hue (Mk 12:18-27). This in no way belittles the challenges now for someone with a homosexual orientation, but it does suggest that our sexuality (both homosexual and heterosexual) lies with God's story from creation to the renewal of creation.

Second, Sherlock attempts to explain away Paul's revulsion at homosexual acts in a number of ways. She writes: "In verses 26-27 Paul describes behaviour driven by lust and greed rather than committed and faithful love."[198] The problem is that this is plainly false. The persons here are driven by defiance and idolatry into shameful and impure sexual deeds. Paul does not contrast said persons, even implicitly, with committed and monogamous same-sex relationships. As a Greek-speaking Roman citizen, who moved freely between the cities of the eastern Mediterranean, Paul would have come across men and women involved in long-term same-sex relationships. For instance, the Roman Emperor Hadrian was explicitly and publicly homosexual and had a long-term relationship with his partner Antonous before the latter accidentally drowned. The love letters of Philostratus speak of a mix of erotic and romantic love towards a younger man. There are even magical papyri where someone tries to put love spells on someone of the same gender. Martii Nissinen is also clear on this: "Paul does not mention *tribades* or *kinaidoi*, that is, female and male persons who were habitually involved in homoerotic relationships, but if he knew about them (and there is every reason to believe that he did), it is difficult to think that, because of their apparent 'orientation,' he would not have included them in Romans 1:24-27 ... For him, there is no individual inversion or inclination that would make this conduct less culpable ... Presumably nothing would have made Paul approve homoerotic behaviour."[199] Paul, much like every other Jewish author of his time who wrote on the subject, rejected same-

---

198.   Sherlock, "Reading Romans as Anglicans," 40.

199.   Martii Nissinen, *Homoeroticism in the Biblical World: A Historical Perspective* (Minneapolis: Fortress, 1998), 109-12.

sex acts as symptomatic of alienation from God irrespective of the relationship status between the two people. Thus, it is special pleading to assume that Paul was somehow ignorant of committed same-sex relationships.

Sherlock also thinks that Paul here "condemns heterosexual people who are acting, out of greed and lust, *as if they had a homosexual orientation*."[200] Once more this is simply not the case. Paul does not censure a gay fiction of straight men and women performing homosexual acts as inflamed by excessive lust. Paul exhibits disapproval at female-female and male-male sexual acts regardless of the sexual preference of the partners. It would be anachronistic to expect Paul to be aware of modern insights into sexual orientation, but Graeco-Roman authors did offer explanations for homosexual behaviour including natural disposition from birth, psychological abnormalities, sexual abuse, or even gender confusion.[201] David Greenberg states: "Physiological explanations for homosexual desire or distinct homosexual roles have a long pedigree, dating back to the world of classical antiquity. Psychological explanations are not exactly new either."[202] So it is naïve to assume that Paul was ignorant of lifelong homosexual partnerships or that Paul had no awareness of homosexuality as related to psychological, social, or biological factors.

Furthermore, the idea that same-sex acts and relationships were normal, natural, and beneficial had been argued in the Graeco-Roman world long before Alfred Kinsey. For instance, Philostratus complained that a boy who failed to respond to his advances was "opposing the commands of nature."[203] Achilles Tatius asserted

---

200. Sherlock, "Reading Romans as Anglicans,"41 (italics added).

201. Hubbard, *Homosexuality in Greece and Rome* 165; Gagnon, *Bible and Homosexual Practice* 385.

202. David F. Greenberg, *The Construction of Homosexuality* (Chicago: University of Chicago Press, 1988), 485.

203. Philostratus, *Ep.* 64.

that kisses from a boy were "of nature."[204] Paul was undoubtedly exposed in Graeco-Roman culture to philosophical apologies for homosexual love and homosexual acts, and yet he makes no concession for certain types of homosexuality nor does he mitigate his remarks by careful qualification.

Third, Sherlock's appeal to Galatians 3:28 ("There is no longer Jew or Greek, there is no longer slave or free, there is no longer male and female; for all of you are one in Christ Jesus") as applicable to gay and straight folks is as predictable as it is laboured. She writes: "If we are indeed all one in Christ, then there is no male or female, just as there is no slave or free, and no gay or straight. If we now wish to make the words of Paul himself into a new Law, we are doing what the apostle fiercely condemned."[205] Now if Sherlock thinks that binding oneself to any law or constellation of ethical obligations is somehow legalistic, then we suggest she keep reading on to Galatians 5–6, especially with Paul's exhortation to fulfil "the Law of Christ" (Gal 6:2). Moreover, we doubt that gay and straight is a binary opposition that Paul would willingly include in his coordinated set of negations in Galatians 3:28. In Galatians, Paul is again appealing to the story of creation using the biological terminology for "male" and "female" as he has done in Romans 1:26-27. His argument is indeed one of inclusion, but this is of all peoples created by God, regardless of how society ranked and classified them. Sherlock is right that this includes the homosexual community too, but what she misreads is that Galatians 3:28 is not a magic hermeneutical wand that is a "free pass" to enable us to create God's world in our own image. By repeatedly alluding to the creational and covenantal narratives in Galatians, Paul is doing the exact opposite, he is drawing the Galatians' attention back to the theocentric essence of redemptive-history where God and not humanity is at the centre. An anthropocentric reading such as Sherlock's misreads the text and her suggestion that moving

---

204. Achilles Tatius, *Leuc. Clit.* 2.38.

205. Sherlock, "Reading Romans as Anglicans," 42.

gays and lesbians into the centre will solve current hermeneutical tensions is inherently flawed. Paul comes to his universal statement in Galatians 3:28 from the metaphor in Galatians 3:27 that we are now clothed with Christ Jesus. What does this clothing look like? Can it be any designer cut?

Paul begins and indeed centres Galatians 3 on the story of Abraham, which makes clear that God's desire is to bless all people (Gen 12:3), hence his universal statement in 3:28. Yet when God called Abram and Sarai, he called them to live lives that reflected the character and nature of God. In doing this, they became a light to the Gentiles, a beacon reflecting God's grace. The love of God *is* inclusive of all people, but this inclusion does not mean, and never did mean, that it is a license to live any way we choose. There are boundaries, there always were, and we suggest there always will be. Paul goes on to a sample list of such limits in Galatians 5:16-21 which begins with a sexual boundary, and then lists the fruit of the Spirit-empowered life which characterise those who are clothed with Christ. Sherlock's desire to find a scriptural basis for living a homosexual lifestyle from both Galatians 3:28 and Romans 1:26-27 is consistently found at odds with her intention to read and listen to the whole of Scripture.[206] Scripture repeatedly affirms God's gift of sex within the bounds of marriage between a man and a woman.

Fourth, Sherlock in the end reveals her primary argument when, following Walter Wink, she advocates that the Bible has no sexual ethic, only a variety of sexual mores that fluctuate over time and vary through cultures. Instead, we are told, the Bible knows only an ethic of love, which is constantly brought to bear upon whatever sexual mores are prevailing.[207]The move is exceptionally disingenuous as she eliminates the applicability and authority of every single biblical commandment about sexuality in Christian Scripture by relativising it against its own background. This is an unhelpful line of argumentation for several reasons. (1) By restricting

---

206. Sherlock, "Reading Romans as Anglicans," 34-35.

207. Sherlock, "Reading Romans as Anglicans," 42-43.

the relevance of each biblical command about sexuality to the bounds of its own cultural milieu, Sherlock is conveniently creating a vacuum where biblical sexual ethics have no prescription at all, and one can therefore freely construct any sexual ethic one likes and it becomes self-justifying as long as one can somehow demonstrate that it is "loving." (2) But let us play Devil's Advocate and ask if there really is a single biblical love ethic. If we adopt the same relativity towards a biblical love ethic that Sherlock applies to biblical statements about sexuality, then we forfeit any way to coherently ground ethical behaviour. After all, what is "loving" in Bronze Age Canaan, or in exilic Babylon, or first century Galilee, or mid-first century Corinth can hardly be uniform. Is divorcing and expelling foreign wives a loving act? Or what about expecting a girl to regain her honour by marrying her rapist because no other man will now want her? Who determines what is "loving" behaviour? (3) We also remain concerned that Sherlock has forfeited any grounds for censuring virtually any kind of non-violent sexual behaviour. If we adopt her program of biblical relativity plus undefined love ethic, then it is impossible to censure promiscuity, polyamory, or polygamy without falling under the weight of her own criticism of legalism. In other words, Sherlock has paved the way for a sexual ethic that does not have the moral courage to say "no" to anything other than the most deplorable acts of sexual violence. This runs counter to Jesus, God-in-the-flesh, who was quite happy to say "no" and set boundaries on human sexual behaviour (e.g. Matt 5:27-32; 15:19; 19:18-19).

Reading Romans 1:26-27 as Anglicans

So how are Anglicans to read Romans 1:26-27? We want to suggest four factors for consideration.

1.   On inclusiveness, we are unsure what Sherlock means when she suggests that we bring gays and lesbians from the margins to the centre. If by that she means practising hospitality, listening, loving, and sharing in a local church context, we are in full agreement. But we suspect she means something more in terms of validate and ordain to holy orders, something we hesitate at. A better model,

something in line with Richard Burridge's suggestion, is that we practise hermeneutical inclusivity where we willingly read, mark, learn, and digest Scripture together in order to better understand Scripture and each other too.[208] Furthermore, while the Christian community is indeed radically inclusive as it follows the example of Jesus, it is also a redemptive and transformative community. Because "all have sinned," everyone without exception –Jew and Gentile, slave and free, gay and straight– everyone needs the redemption that comes from the cross of Christ, the new life that flows from the resurrection of Christ, and the transformation that ebbs from the work of Holy Spirit. So everyone is invited to church, and come as you are, but no one is allowed to stay as they are.[209]

2.   On listening, this is vitally important and along with Sherlock we hold to its importance. But listening to gay and lesbian experience cannot be one way. Those of us engaging in this conversation on the subject of God, sexuality, holiness, and struggle, should also listen to our forefathers and foremothers in the faith, the Global South, celibate gay and lesbian Christians, and even ex-gays as well. At this crucial time in the Anglican Communion we must make sure we hear the full spectrum of voices from the global church and not marginalise voices we don't like by displaying a colonial attitude that projects superior knowledge or sophistication by the white-western world. Let us seek to exhibit a truly catholic practice as we listen.

3.   On ecumenical challenges, much thought should be given to how a full acceptance and affirmation of homosexuality will affect relationships with other churches. The episcopacy is meant to be a symbol of ecclesiological unity and theological integrity, yet the homosexuality debate has led to episcopal disunity perpetuated by a failure to uphold the faith delivered to the saints. The pursuit of unity with Catholic, Orthodox, and Protestant churches will be

---

208.   Richard Burridge, *Imitating Jesus: An Inclusive Approach to New Testament Ethics* (Grand Rapids, MI: Eerdmans, 2005), 395.

209.   We owe this latter point to Dr. Ben Witherington of Asbury Theological Seminary.

irreversibly damaged if the ordination of practising homosexuals to the episcopacy continues. Moreover, within the Anglican Communion itself, we face the problem that Lambeth Resolution 1.10 sets out the official position of the Anglican Communion on sexuality[210] while many provinces continue to willfully defy it with impunity. The attempt of the Anglican Covenant to fix this problem is dead in the water as even the English Church has not accepted it. It would seem that we are left with either repealing Resolution 1.10 or else adopting a two-tier Anglican Communion.

4.   On ordination, I (Sarah) as an ordained Anglican woman in the evangelical tradition would like to affirm again that the debate around the ordination of women must not be confused with the ordination of practising gays and lesbians as is alluded to by Sherlock in her chapter on Romans and by Kirby in his introduction. If we accept that Romans 1 possesses a deliberate echo of the creation story, then on a very foundational level we need to recognise that God is imaged by both male and female (Gen 1:26-27) and this "imaging" should provide the presupposition to our reading about humanity in Romans 1. It is not only males, but male and female who constitute the image of God, indicating that the complementarity of men and women is essential for projecting the image of God into the world; yet such complementarity does not exist in same-sex relationships. That is not to say that the church has always grasped the importance of male and female partnership and gospel equality; many versions of Christian patriarchy are demeaning to women. Yet the attempt to establish a trajectory from women's ordination to the full acceptance of practising homosexuality fails because the latter cannot be reconciled with the interpersonal connectedness of men and women as custodians of creation and covenant partners with God in the canon.

Scripture in its propositional affirmations, narrative framework, and eschatological telos simply does not allow for the inclusiveness that the authors of *Five Uneasy Pieces* crave. That does not mean that

---

210.   See the Lambeth Conference Official Website. http://www.lambethconference.org/resolutions/1998/1998-1-10.cfm.

the opportunity for ordination is closed for persons with same-sex attraction. For celibate single homosexuals, as with celibate single heterosexuals, the door is of course open if God calls them and the church recognises that call. I realise that I, as an ordained woman, have had a door opened for me that the homosexual community now want widened for themselves, and I have considerable empathy for the frustration and confusion that may be felt by this community. However as an Anglican scholar committed to the truth of Scripture and with Jesus as the North Star, I can find no place in Scripture within which the church can find room to move on this issue.

Conclusion

Roman Catholic biblical scholar Luke Timothy Johnson writes about the Scripture and Homosexuality debate: "I have little patience with efforts to make Scripture say something other than what it says, through appeals to linguistic or cultural subtleties. The exegetical situation is straightforward: we know what the text says. But what are we to *do* with what the text says?" When it comes to the matter of the scriptural teaching on homosexuality, Johnson is brutally honest: "I think it important to state clearly that we do, in fact, reject the straightforward commands of Scripture, and appeal instead to another authority when we declare that same-sex unions can be holy and good. We appeal explicitly to the weight of our own experience and the experience thousands of others have witnessed to, which tells us that to claim our own sexual orientation is in fact to accept the way in which God has created us."[211] Personally, we find Johnson's position far more candid and consistent than Sherlock's. For Johnson, Scripture is something that is negotiable, but Sherlock is clumsily struggling to make the text endorse precisely what it censures. We would point out that Article 20 of the Articles of Religion in the *Book of Common Prayer* (1662) urges us not to "ordain any thing that is contrary to God's Word written." The real question is not really what Paul says, it is a question of whether

---

211. Luke Timothy Johnson, "Scripture & Experience," *Commonweal*. http://commonwealmagazine.org/homosexuality-church-1. Dated 15 June 2007. Cited 13 April 2012.

we as Anglicans and as Christians will be people of Scripture, or people who deny what Scripture teaches and expects of us. The debate in the Anglican Communion is not primarily about what men and women do with their genitals, it is about the authority of the God who speaks in Scripture through his Spirit. We pray that we find grace in the boundaries God sets for us and so live abundantly in God's presence; we leave you with the benediction of Paul to the Romans.

> Now to God who is able to strengthen you according to my gospel and the proclamation of Jesus Christ, according to the revelation of the mystery that was kept secret for long ages but is now disclosed, and through the prophetic writings is made known to all the Gentiles, according to the command of the eternal God, to bring about the obedience of faith— to the only wise God, through Jesus Christ, to whom be the glory forever! Amen. (Rom 16:25-27 NRSV).

CHAPTER 5

God, Creation and Sexuality in First Corinthians: A Response to Alan Cadwallader

PAUL BARNETT

Synopsis

Does Paul refer to homoerotic activity in 1 Corinthians 6:9-11? This short paper argues that Paul in fact does, in response to Alan Cadwallader[212] who argues that he does not. My understanding, however, is that Paul was not conducting an intentional attack on such behaviour, but rather saw it as unacceptably inconsistent with three interconnected entities - the unity of God, the unity of creation, and the unity of monogamous heterosexual marriage.

A. Argument and response

To begin let me identify and comment on some of Alan Cadwallader's key points.

(i) Role of biblical texts

According to Cadwallader, the "biblical texts do have a critical part to play in the formation of attitudes, beliefs and behaviours..." (p. 47).

Comment: This rather qualified viewpoint falls short of Paul's own assertion in this epistle, "If anyone thinks he is a prophet or spiritual, he should acknowledge that the things I am *writing* to you [Corinthians] are *a command* of the Lord" (1 Cor 14:37). Paul's writings carry the force and divine authority of Sacred Scripture.

(ii) Gradations of context

Alan Cadwallader states that "there is a need to set a part of the biblical text into the gradations of context that successively circle that text" (p. 47).

Comment: This appears to suggest that we *circle* down into our key text from wider extremities. It soon becomes apparent that Alan Cadwallader sees the context of 1 Corinthians 6:9-11 determined by the scandalous situation in 1 Corinthians 5:1-2.

I defer for the moment further discussion of this until Alan

---

212.   Alan Cadwallader, "Keeping Lists or Embracing Freedom: 1 Corinthians 6:9–10 in Context" in *Five Uneasy Pieces: Essays on Scripture and Sexuality* (Adelaide: ATF Press, 2011), Chapter 4.

Cadwallader more directly raises it. I am uncomfortable with the idea that we "circle" down from a wider context into a specific text. To the contrary, Paul moves step-by-step progressively through his pastoral concerns, in a *linear* way, as it were, which he expected his readers to follow, acknowledge and adopt.

(iii)   Incest

An important part of Alan Cadwallader's argument is that "the man who has his father's wife" (5:2) represents a case of incest (p. 57). He builds his argument on that assumption (pp. 57-61).

Comment: Of course, the "sexual immorality" may have been incest (condemned in Lev 18:7-8), but equally it may have been a situation involving the man's *stepmother*[213] with whom the man and his father were both sexually engaged. Scholars are divided.[214] It is precarious to build an argument on an uncertain foundation.

(iv)   The meaning of keywords[215]

Cadwallader says "the etymological argument – often taken as determining the intent of this verse is completely invalid" (49). Here he refers to the critical words in our passage, *malakoi* and *arsenokoitai* (1 Cor 6:9). *Comment*: I think this overstates the case because sometimes the etymology and the meaning coincide.

(a)   *Malakos* literally means "soft", as in "a man in soft clothing" (Matt 11:8), but by usage it also means "soft", "effeminate" as of "being passive in a same-sex relationship" (BDAG)[216]. Cadwallader, however, argues that changing word meanings preclude certainty

---

213.   Condemned in Deuteronomy 27:20?

214.   For example, C.K. Barrett, *The First Epistle to the Corinthians* (London: A&C Black, 1973), 121 identifies the woman as the stepmother.

215.   Linda Belleville, "The Challenges of Translating Ἀρσενοκοῖται and Μαλακοί in 1 Cor 6:9: A Reassessment in Light of Koine Greek and First-Century Cultural Mores". *The Bible Translator* 62(2011) 22-29.

216.   F.W. Danker (Rev and Ed) *A Greek-English Lexicon of the New Testament and Other Early Christian Literature* based on previous English editions by Arndt, Gingrich and Danker (Chicago: Chicago University Press, 2000).

of the meaning of *malakos* in 1 Corinthians 6:9.

Comment: In Aristophanes's play, *Clouds*, the corruption of Athens is linked to the effeminacy of the youth who "make their voices soft/effeminate [*malakēn*] for a lover, marching around pimping themselves".[217] Paul's contemporary, the Jew Philo in his discussion of homosexual behaviour (*Special Laws* 3.37-42), applies *malakos* to the behaviour of passive sexual partners generally, behaviour that was not confined to "call boys".[218]

(b)   According to BAGD *arsenokoitēs* means "a male who engages in sexual activity with a person of his own sex". Whilst the word occurs first in extant literature in this text (1 Cor 6:9), and with due deference to the importance of context in determining meaning, the constituent parts of the word leave little doubt about that meaning. Because *arsēn* means "man" and *koitai* means "lying" the combination of the two in one word means "a man lying with a man". This is supported by the Greek Old Testament's rendering of Leviticus 18:22 – "Thou shalt not lie [*koitēn*] with a man [*arsenos*] as with a woman, for it is an abomination" (also Lev 20:13).

The location of these two words together points to the sexual act between two men, one the passive partner (*malakos*), the other the active partner (*arsenokoitēs*).[219]

---

217.   Cited in B. Thornton, *Eros. The Myth of Ancient Greek Sexuality* (Boulder: HarperCollins, 1997), 118. Thornton's thesis is that contrary to modern opinion, the Greeks in the classical era felt threatened by the engulfing chaos of rampant heterosexual promiscuity and male-to-male sexuality. He points out the routinely used word for the passive homosexual is *kinaidos*. Nonetheless, Aristophanes's use of **malakēn** for the passive partner (as above) is evidence that Paul's *malakoi* is to be understood in that sense.

218.   See further R.A.J. Gagnon, *The Bible and Homosexual Practice* (Nashville: Abingdon Press, 2001), 308-309.

219.   Gagnon, *Homosexual Practice* 315-332 demonstrates against Scroggs, Martin and others that Paul is not referring to abusive or exploitative sexual practices against the *malakoi*.

(v)   Vice lists

Cadwallader makes extensive references to "vice lists" as they occur in the New Testament and broadly contemporary literature. He states that "it is clear that the specific vices of a list may have no direct case example among either an audience or in a derogated group or individual" (p. 55). In other words – if I interpret Cadwallader correctly – he is saying that the vice lists in First Corinthians (5:11 and 6:9-10) are stereotypical and general and not descriptive of Paul's readers in Corinth at the time he wrote this letter.

Comment: This view is not borne out by the contexts of these passages.

(a) In 1 Corinthians 5:11 Paul is correcting the Corinthians' misunderstanding of an earlier, now-lost letter. They thought he meant they must "not...associate with sexually immoral people" in society at large (v. 11) whereas – as he now indicates – it was "not to eat with" the *one who is named a "brother"* (fellow-Christian).

Actually, v. 11 is an *inclusio*[220] framed by "not to associate with" (*synanamignysthai* – "mingle with") and "not...to eat with" (*synesthiein* – "eat together with"). The framing verbs point to sharing life together in the faith-community including eating together, a possible allusion to the Lord's Supper.

> But now I am writing to you
> *not to associate with* anyone who bears the name of brother
> if he is guilty of
>> sexual immorality
>> or greed,
>> or is an idolater,
>> reviler,
>> drunkard,
>> or swindler
> *not* even *to eat with* such a one.

---

220. A parallel or double "book-end" to a section, ending where it began.

Rather than regard v. 11 as an undifferentiated "vice list" it is better to understand its items as examples of *concrete* and *public* evils by church members, which said Paul, would preclude their continuing presence at the public meetings of believers.

At the head of the list is the very public "sexually immoral man" (*pornos*) who was sexually engaged with his father's wife (5:1). The other items apply to Corinthian church members whose lives in the wider community are a matter of moral shame as well as a source of corruption within the church ("a little leaven leavens the whole lump" – 5:6). The congregation is to subject them to the discipline of exclusion ("not...associate with"/ "not...eat with") ahead of their hoped for repentance and restoration.

(b)   1 Corinthians 6:9-10 is also an *inclusio,* framed by "inherit the kingdom of God".

Or do you not know that the unrighteous will not inherit the kingdom of God?

> Do not be deceived:
> neither the sexually immoral,
> nor idolaters,
> nor adulterers,
> nor men who practice homosexuality (*oute malakoi oute arsenokoitai*[221])
> nor thieves,
> nor the greedy,
> nor drunkards,
> nor revilers,
> nor swindlers will inherit the kingdom of God.

The framing warnings about "not/inheriting the kingdom of God" indicate that this is no mere abstract "vice list" but the apostle's practical pastoral warning to the Corinthian believers to repent

---

221.   ESV, rather than directly translating the two nouns, interprets them as "men who practice homosexuality", assuming the male homosexual act; likewise RSV ("sexual perverts"). Other versions preserve the two entities, e.g.,: NRSV ("male prostitutes...sodomites"); NIV ("male prostitutes...homosexual offenders"); TNIV ("nor male prostitutes...practicing homosexuals").

of such behaviours. There is a connection between the pastoral admonitions ("not to associate with"/ "not to eat with") and the pastoral warnings of eschatological exclusion ("will not inherit the kingdom of God"). Exclusion from the congregation coincides with and points to exclusion from the kingdom.

I agree with Cadwallader in finding a connection between the two lists (p. 58). The second list repeats the six items of the first list, but now stated as plurals. Both lists begin with "the sexually immoral" (*pornos/pornoi*) and probably spring from the case of the notorious sexual offender in 5:1-2.

The second list, like the first, is focused on *specific* behaviour by the believers in Corinth. The words immediately (v. 11) following clinch the point:

> And such *were* some of you.
> But   you were *washed*,
>   you were *sanctified*,
>   you were *justified*
>   in the name of the Lord Jesus Christ and
>   by the Spirit of our God.

The verb tenses are critical. "Such *were* (ēte) some of you" is imperfective, indicating the habitual and routine manner of life of "some", which is contrasted by a series of perfectives (aorist passives) each introduced by the strong adversative "but" (*alla*). These are real people in the Corinthian church who *had been engaged* in "unrighteous" lifestyles, but who had been "washed" (in baptism), "sanctified" (by the Spirit) and "justified" (in Christ), whose lives have been radically changed. This is no stereotypical list, but a historical *description* of the effects of the radical power of God in the lives of these Corinthians.[222]

---

222. Likewise Paul's reference to the Corinthians' "quarrelling, jealousy, anger, hostility, slander, gossip, conceit, disorder" is no mere formal list but his description of actual behaviour by some at Paul's second visit (2 Cor 12:20).

(vi)   *The identification of the offender in 1 Corinthians 5:1-2 with the malakoi and arsenokoitai in 1 Corinthians 6:9.*

What, then, are we to think about the four extra behaviours noted in the second list — the "adulterers" (*moichoi*), "men who practice homosexuality" (*malakoi* and *arsenokoitai*), and "thieves" (*kleptai*)? We may eliminate "adulterers" and "thieves" since their activities are clear enough. This leaves us with the *malakoi* and the *arsenokoitai*.

Alan Cadwallader has a very specific point of view on these keywords (pp. 57-61). He argues that *malakoi* and the *arsenokoitai* refer allusively to the person involved in the scandalous behaviour in 5:1-2 — the incestuous man.

Fundamental to his exposition is his assertion "it is clear that the configuration of *incest* is still operating" (p. 58; my italics). He then makes a connection between incest and Philo's understanding of *malakos* as "loss of manhood", which he conjoins with "adultery and pandering". In short, Cadwallader effectively identifies the incestuous son (in 5:2) with the *malakos* (in 6:9). He concludes, "The parallels with Paul's vice list are patent" (p. 58).[223]

In similar vein he connects the **arsenokoitēs** with the specific case in 5:1-2. He argues (1) "the wife of the man's father is...an extension of the father"; and (2) "to sleep in another man's bed" is "euphemism" for incest. Thus, as I understand Cadwallader,[224] he is implying that son who has lain with his father's wife is also the *arsenokoitēs*.

Comment: I have several problems with Cadwallader's reconstruction. First, his argument is tenuous. He reads Paul's text through the lens of extraneous and unrelated vice lists like Philo's rather than pursuing a direct, "common sense" reading of the apostle's exposition in chapters 5-6. Second, his connection of the two keywords with the concrete case in 5:1-2 is imaginative, but speculative. Thirdly, his general argument is idiosyncratic and does

---

223. Cadwallader gives no cross-reference in support of this view.

224. This paper was prepared at the eleventh hour and there was no opportunity to check with Alan Cadwallader about the intent of this section of his paper.

not appear (to my knowledge) in mainstream authorities.

(vii)   The place of law in the writings of Paul

Cadwallader observes that, based on Galatians and Romans, "law...understood as negative regulations or merit-delivering works could never deliver a person. Hence to ground a warning against *porneia* (sexual immorality) in a legal injunction was to return to the condition from which Jesus had liberated people" (p. 61).

Comment: Jesus and the apostles repeatedly reaffirm the moral law as in the second table of commandments. Christ crucified and resurrected is, indeed, the only way to know and be known by God and be blessed by the presence of the Spirit of his Son. Equally, however, the now "justified" person is to "live out" the Christian "walk" in the holiness expressed in those commandments. Paul repeatedly warns that those who breach these Christianised statements of the commandments "will not inherit the kingdom of God" (1 Cor 6:9, 10; Gal 5:21).

(viii)   A vice list in the Parable of the Pharisee and the Tax Collector (Luke 18:9-14)?

Cadwallader notes that the three things the Pharisee thanked God he was not (an "extortioner", "unjust", an "adulterer") also occur in 1 Corinthians 6:9-11 (pp. 61-62). He finds the coincidence "striking" and suggests the possibility that "Luke has Paul as the source of his vice list" (p. 62). Cadwallader's point is that Christian leaders (and others) who pass judgment on people as unrighteous — including in matters relating to sexual practices — may be acting like the Pharisee in the parable. He "wonders" if "the Corinthian propensity for misunderstanding Paul was a virus in the early church and Luke felt compelled to bring a dominical corrective to bear".

Comment: Is there any reason to doubt that the words Jesus ascribed to the Pharisee were not historically true? Is Cadwallader suggesting that this is not a parable of Jesus that Luke is narrating but a parable of and by *Luke*? Such was the reverence of disciples of Jesus for their Lord that I find it difficult to believe they felt free to put their words in the mouth of the historical Jesus. In any case, a Pharisee may well have regarded tax collectors as extortioners, unjust and adulterers, and been justified in doing so.

B. Pluralism in Corinth and Paul's adaptation of the Shema'

Corinth, like other cities in the Graeco-Roman world, was *pluralist* in religion, with "many 'gods' and many 'lords'" (1 Cor 8:5). Pausanias, the travel writer who visited Corinth some time after Paul, describes numerous temples and shrines to a bewildering array of deities in Corinth's public square (*agora*).[225]

In First Corinthians Paul adapts the *Shema'* ("Hear, O Israel, the Lord your God is *one*" – Deut 6:4) to express Yahweh's revelation of himself as *the Father* of Jesus his Son who is *the Lord*.

> there is _one_ God, the Father,
> > from whom are all things...
> and
> > _one_ Lord, Jesus Christ,
> > > through whom are all things...
> (1 Cor 8:6).

In other words, Paul's gospel was focused on the one-ness of the Father ("*from* whom are all things" – i.e., the creation) and the one-ness of the Lord Jesus Christ ("*through* whom are all things" – i.e., the creation).

By contrast the plurality of "gods many, lords many" implied not the one-ness of the creation, but its fundamental *dissonance*, its fragmented-ness. The worship of idols (polytheism) is symptomatic of the sense of creation's autonomy from the Creator (pantheism). The flip side to the apostle's direction to turn to the Father through the Lord Jesus is to "flee from the worship of idols" (1 Cor 10:14). The one action demands the other. This is no mere empty slogan but reflected Paul's "world view" of the one-ness of the Father and the one-ness of the Lord but also the one-ness of the Creation that is *from* the Father *through* the Lord. The preaching of the gospel was

---

225. Pausanias, *Description of Greece*, 2.6-7.

a powerful and challenging cultural alternative to the polytheism and pantheism of Corinth.

C. The Unity of the God and monogamous heterosexual marriage

Two passages in First Thessalonians should be connected.

> ...*you turned to God from idols* to serve the living and true God, and to wait for his Son from heaven, whom he raised from the dead, Jesus who delivers us from the wrath to come (1:9-10).

> Finally, then, brothers, we ask and urge you in the Lord Jesus, that as you received from us how you ought to walk and to please God, just as you are doing, that you do so more and more. For you know what instructions we gave you through the Lord Jesus. For this is the will of God, your sanctification: that you abstain *from sexual immorality (porneia)*; that each one of you knows how to control his own body in holiness and honour (4:1-4).

The "turning" to God from the "many gods" demands at the same time a radical moral "turning". In the culture of "many gods" there was the acceptance of many sexual partners. The temples of the many gods were the temples of multiple sexual encounters. But the "turning" to the God who is *one* required the commitment to *one* heterosexual spouse and to the care of the children of that union. Closely connected to this new commitment was the "work ethic" by which parents took responsibility to provide for their families.

Marital fidelity for the *whole* of life as an ethical response to the unity of God in creation and redemption occurs repeatedly in the Pauline corpus, no doubt reflecting Paul's preaching and catechesis.

D. God and Sexuality

Twice in First Corinthians Paul enjoins the church to "flee" – from sexual immorality (*porneia* – 6:18) and idolatry (*eidōlatreia* – 10:14). Both were symptoms of the dissonance of "things" and people unconnected with the Father and the Lord. Homosexual practices are just one example of disconnected dissonance. This is the reason Paul views them so negatively (Rom 1:18-32; 1 Cor 6:9), but no more so than heterosexual adultery. Turning to the "one" God from idols also and equally means for those who engage in sexual practices the turning to one heterosexual spouse. Paul's negativity towards homosexual practices is the flip side of his positivity about heterosexual marriage that in turn expresses his view of the unity of the Creation that is from the Father and through the Lord.

E. Conclusion

First, contrary to Alan Cadwallader, I argue that we must read texts like 1 Corinthians 5-6 in a direct, linear, commonsense way. Contemporary sources – like Philo – are not where we start, but rather the apostolic text. Only when we have mastered the apostolic text by the good principles of exegesis (context, organic structure and grammatical and verbal analysis) do we turn to "secular" sources to elucidate further the biblical text.

Secondly, in my view – and with respect – I do not believe that Cadwallader has made his case about the meanings of the two keywords (*malakos* and *arsenokoitēs*), both of which point to coital intercourse.

Thirdly, the "vice lists", while appearing to be stereotypical are actually descriptive of aspects of morality in Corinth that were being expressed within the faith community.

Fourthly, Paul's starting point is not his criticism of homoerotic activity but his advocacy of heterosexual monogamous marriage as the only appropriate expression of sexuality based on the unity (not dissonance) of the Creation that is "from the one Father" and "through the one Lord".

CHAPTER 6

The Moral Usefulness of the Law: 1 Timothy 1:8-11

DENISE COOPER-CLARKE

We know that the law is good if one uses it properly. We also know that the law is made not for the righteous but for lawbreakers and rebels, the ungodly and sinful, the unholy and irreligious, for those who kill their fathers or mothers, for murderers, for the sexually immoral, for those practicing homosexuality, for slave traders and liars and perjurers. And it is for whatever else is contrary to the sound doctrine that conforms to the gospel concerning the glory of the blessed God, which he entrusted to me. (1Tim 1:8-11 TNIV)[226]

Introduction

In his foreword to *Five Uneasy Pieces*, William Countryman challenges those who take a "conservative" stance on the morality of homosexual acts to "articulate our fundamental presuppositions in ways that are intelligible to one another," and to "lay out, with a clarity comparable to that presented here exactly how and why they interpret the texts as they do."[227] This is what I will attempt to do in responding to the progressive reading of 1 Timothy 1:8-11 by Gregory Jenks.[228]

Revisionist Arguments Based on Exegesis

Arguments for what I shall call a "revisionist" position on homosexuality may be divided into two broad types, though they are frequently combined by individual writers. Early revisionist works by Anglican priest Derrick Sherwin Bailey,[229] Catholic historian John

---

226. I have used the translation of the TNIV (Today's New International Version) as it is the best of the recent translations and far better than that of the NRSV for this text.

227. L. William Countryman, "Foreword. Scripture, Homosexuality and Anglicans: Creating a Conversation," in *Five Uneasy Pieces* (Adelaide: ATF Press, 2011), xi-xvii, xiii, xvii.

228. Gregory C. Jenks, "Rules for Holy Living: A Progressive Reading of 1 Timothy 1:8-11," in *Five Uneasy Pieces* (Adelaide: ATF Press, 2011), 69-83.

229. Derrick S. Bailey, *Homosexuality and the Western Christian Tradition* (London: Longmans Green, 1955).

Boswell,[230] and New Testament scholar Robin Scroggs,[231] sought to show that the scriptural passages which had traditionally been read to disallow all homosexual acts had been misinterpreted, and that they were irrelevant to the question of the morality of faithful, loving homosexual relationships. This type of argument is about the exegesis (exploration of the original meaning) of certain texts, and is based on understanding the meaning of terms, the genre of the text, and the historical, cultural and theological context. Such an approach is consistent with the high view of Scripture held by Evangelical, and many Roman Catholic and Eastern Orthodox believers, namely, that Scripture (rightly interpreted) is the primary authority for Christian faith and practice. The question then becomes whether these revisionist readings are exegetically valid.

Examples of such revisionist arguments include the assertion that the Old Testament law proscribing male homosexual acts (Lev 18:22 and 20:13) has to do with ritual purity rather than morality,[232] or that an association with idolatry is the reason for the prohibition of male homosexual acts,[233] or that the underlying principle behind the whole of Leviticus 18 is "procreation within a stable family."[234] In relation to Romans 1:26-27, Scroggs claimed that Paul was referring only to pederasty (men having sex with boys) and Boswell avers that he was referring only to same-sex behaviour by those who were "naturally" that is, by orientation, heterosexual.[235] And there is

---

230. John Boswell, *Christianity, Social Tolerance and Homosexuality* (Chicago: University of Chicago Press, 1980).

231. Robin Scroggs, *The New Testament and Homosexuality: Contextual Background for Contemporary Debate* (Philadelphia: Fortress Press, 1983).

232. Boswell, *Christianity, Social Tolerance and Homosexuality* 100-102.

233. Richard Treloar, "On 'Not Putting New Wine into Old Wineskins', or 'Taking the Bible Fully Seriously': An Anglican Reading of Leviticus 18:22 and 20:13," in *Five Uneasy Pieces* (Adelaide: ATF Press, 2011), 13-30.

234. Jacob Milgrom, *Leviticus 17-22: A New Translation and Commentary* (New York: Doubleday, 2000), 1568.

235. Scroggs, *The New Testament and Homosexuality* 16, 116-117; Boswell, *Christianity, Social Tolerance and Homosexuality* 112-113.

debate about the meaning of the term *arsenokoitai* in 1 Corinthians 6:9-10 and 1 Timothy 1:8-11, traditionally construed as men who have sexual relations with other men. Yet the consensus among both conservative and even many revisionist scholars is that these readings are not well founded.[236]

Revisionist Arguments Based on Hermeneutics

There are other revisionist approaches, based not on exegesis (the original meaning of the text), but on hermeneutics (the way of framing the text for the contemporary situation). Conservative scholars are not committed to "wooden" readings. We acknowledge that in relation to ethical issues, we cannot uncritically transfer any one scriptural text directly to our present day context. But one of our presuppositions is that "[t]he meaning of a specific scriptural passage *then* has a controlling influence on its meaning *now*." This is "the initial defense against 'eisegesis' (reading meaning into the text) which twists the text to say whatever the reader wishes."[237] Another presupposition is that we need to consider the biblical witness as a whole, the entire horizon of the biblical story, in order to discern and differentiate the intrinsic and abiding moral principles from what is historically or culturally conditioned when it comes to understanding what is ethical behaviour for believers today. In other words, to adopt the canonical approach to the reading of Scripture, commended by Article XX of the *Book of Common Prayer*, in which "its various parts are understood in light of a sense of the whole, such that Scripture is read coherently." [238]

---

236. See, for example, Roy E. Ciampa and Brian S. Rosner, *The First Letter to the Corinthians* (Grand Rapids, Michigan: Eerdmans, 2010), Robert A.J. Gagnon, *The Bible and Homosexual Practice* (Nashville: Abingdon Press, 2001, Richard B. Hays, *The Moral Vision of the New Testament: Community, Cross, New Creation* (New York: Harper One, 1996), Luke Timothy Johnson, "Debate & Discernment: Scripture & the Spirit," *Commonweal* 121/2 (1994): 12-13.

237. William C. Spohn, *What are they Saying About Scripture and Ethics?* (New York and Mahwah, NJ.: Paulist Press, 1995), 6.

238. Treloar, "On 'Not Putting New Wine into Old Wineskins'," 17.

We also need to be able to discern the similarities and differences between our situation and the situation of these ancient texts. There are many ways in which our situation differs from that of the biblical writers, including a far greater knowledge of the natural world provided by modern science, which may challenge past interpretations based on outdated ideas. Further, we need to take seriously the challenge to identify and acknowledge the presuppositions that inevitably shape our reading. "Every inquiry moves to some extent around the 'hermeneutical circle'; that is the data answers the questions we ask and gets massaged into the procedures that we employ. Self-critical awareness of our own perspective (confessional commitments, social location, class, gender, race, nationality, etc.) can prevent this 'hermeneutical circle' from becoming a vicious one."[239] While our presuppositions need some honest and self-critical scrutiny, they are genuinely and deliberately malleable, as we ought to be open to allowing Scripture to challenge and shape them. Finally, we need to recognise that just as the original texts were produced by faith communities, these same texts are to be interpreted in community—the locus of textual meaning is not discerned by isolated individual readers, but in the context of the communion of saints, the evangelical and apostolic community.

Revisionist Arguments Based on "The Whole of Scripture"

So we turn to the second broad type of argument used by revisionist scholars, based on broader hermeneutical considerations. One approach is to argue that, regardless of what the specific scriptural texts which deal with homosexual activity actually say, irrespective of what rules they contain, these rules must either be interpreted to be consistent with the more important general biblical principle of love for neighbour, or, if necessary, simply overridden by it.[240] This

---

239. Spohn, *What are they Saying About Scripture and Ethics?* 8-9.

240. See for example, Walter Wink, "Homosexuality and the Bible" in *Questions of Conscience for the Churches* ed. Walter Wink (Minneapolis: Fortress Press, 1999), 33-49.

approach is in the tradition of situation ethics, which promotes the single biblical principle of love.[241] So, according to New Testament scholar Dale Martin: "[A]ny interpretation of scripture that hurts people, oppresses people, or destroys people cannot be the right interpretation ... If the church wishes to continue with its traditional interpretation it must demonstrate, not just claim, that it is more loving to condemn homosexuality than to affirm homosexuals." [242]

Is it necessarily unloving to believe that certain behaviours are immoral? As John Dickson points out, "We have to ask whether holding a moral view is *in itself* hateful. This is where I think we could learn from the moral genius of Jesus. He was able to be morally exacting and deeply compassionate toward the same people at the same time—though it is a sad and undeniable fact that many in the church since have had difficulty emulating the feat. We ought to be able to love even those with whom we profoundly disagree."[243]

But situation ethics has a tendency to collapse into consequentialism. Martin continues, "Can the church show that same-sex loving relationships damage those involved in them?" and he compares this with the damage (he claims) is done by "consigning thousands of its members to a life of either celibacy or endless psychological manipulations that masquerade as 'healing'?" [244] There is a very real question of whether greater harm is necessarily done by one approach or another,[245] but the mode of ethical reasoning here is

---

241. Joseph Fletcher, *Situation Ethics: The New Morality* (London: SCM, 1966).

242. Dale B. Martin, "Arsenokoitēs and Malakos: Meanings and Consequences" in *Biblical Ethics and Homosexuality: Listening to Scripture* ed. Robert Brawley (Louisville: Westminster John Knox, 1996), 117-136, 130.

243. John Dickson, "Time for some nuance between the Gay and the God-fearing." *ABC News* (2011) http://www.abc.net.au/unleashed/44682.html

244. Martin, "Arsenokoitēs and Malakos: Meanings and Consequences", 131.

245. It is inconsistent with the witness of the New Testament to describe a life of celibacy as a condemnation. The life and testimony of both Jesus and Paul deny the assumption of our culture that sexual experience is indispensable to life in all its fullness, a life of human flourishing. Sexual desire is very powerful but self control is a virtue in all Christians, whether heterosexual or

consequentialist– where consequentialism is the ethical theory that actions are right or wrong solely on the basis of the harm/benefit ratio of the consequences they produce. Biblical ethics is not primarily consequentialist– we are called to obedience, not just to maximising the welfare of the universe.

Another approach is that based on virtue theory, where "the primary focus moves from actions to character, from doing to being, from decisions to dispositions, and from discrete moments to a whole life."[246] James Nelson argues that instead of thinking of sexual sin in terms of certain acts, we should "take motives and dispositions as seriously as the physical acts themselves," and focus on love which is honest, faithful, life-serving, and joyous.[247] There is a strong emphasis on character and the virtues in the Scriptures, but in Christian ethics, principles and virtues (i.e. character traits) are not rivals, but complementary aspects of morality: "principles without traits are impotent and traits without principles are blind."[248]

Revisionist Arguments Based on "New Information"

The approaches above attempt to interpret the teaching of particular texts in the light of the whole of scripture, but there are other revisionist positions which simply say that, while the Old and New Testament writers may well have condemned all homosexual activity, this teaching is no longer authoritative for the church, because we have new information which was unavailable to them.

---

homosexual. In relation to the 'harm' caused by attempts to change sexual orientation, see below.

246. Denise Cooper-Clarke, "Sexuality and the Virtues," in *Whose Homosexuality? Which Authority?* eds. Brian Edgar and Gordon Preece (Adelaide: ATF Press, 2006), 168-186, 171.

247. James Nelson, "The Liberal Approach to Sexual Ethics," in *From Christ to the World* eds. Wayne Boulton, Thomas Kennedy, and Allen Verhey (Grand Rapids: Eerdmans, 1994), 354-358, 357-358.

248. William Frankena, *Ethics* (Englewood Cliffs: Prentice Hall, 1973), 65.

Often the 'new information' appealed to is scientific knowledge. For example, former Justice Michael Kirby says that the churches have got themselves into a "terrible pickle" over human sexuality, and must make the necessary "adjustment to scientific reality".[249] Many people believe that there is scientific evidence that homosexuality is an innate, genetically determined aspect of the human body (the essentialist perspective). But studies indicate that "there is a wide variability in the genetic influence of homosexuality."[250] And even if a tendency to behave in certain ways is innate, this tells us nothing about the morality of the behaviour. Although we are each created in the image of God, sin infects our thinking and our desires more profoundly than we like to admit.

There is also a widespread belief that homosexual orientation is irreversible, and that attempts to reverse it require a profound and destructive denial of the self. However, though change in orientation is difficult and not common, there are some testimonies of genuine change, and while some methods used by Christians have been damaging, attempts to change need not be harmful: "Sexual orientation *can and does* change significantly for some people-those people wanting it and seeking therapy."[251]

Revisionist Arguments Based on "New Revelation"

Others argue that the biblical teaching on homosexual behaviour is no longer authoritative for the church because we have a new revelation from the Spirit through the experience of committed gay or lesbian Christians. Old and New Testament writers may well have condemned all homosexual activity, but this teaching is no longer authoritative for the church, because the new revelation

---

249. Michael Kirby, "Introduction," in *Five Uneasy Pieces* (Adelaide, ATF Press, 2011), xix-xxvi, xix, xxi.

250. The EA Working Group on Human Sexuality, *Beyond Stereotypes* (Box Hill, Victoria: Australian Evangelical Alliance, 2009), 31.

251. *Beyond Stereotypes*, 35.

supersedes not only the Old Testament but also the New.[252] It is argued that just as the early church, faced with evidence of the work of the Holy Spirit in the lives of Gentiles, was forced to rethink its attitude and accept them, so the experience of the work of the Holy Spirit in the lives and ministry of gay/lesbian Christians forces us to rethink our attitudes to same-sex relationships.[253] This is an attractive argument, but I believe it fails for a number of reasons.

First, the debate about homosexuality is not about whether gay and lesbian people can be accepted into the church (they should be), but about the morality of homosexual behaviour. Second, we recognise that we are all flawed but that, thankfully, "God gives the Spirit to broken people (that is, all of us) and ministers grace even through us sinners, without thereby endorsing our sin,"[254] whatever that may be. Third, the experience of gay Christians also includes "those who struggle with homosexual desires and find them a hindrance to living lives committed to the service of God."[255] Finally, the 'conservative' pre-supposition is that experience should be a 'hermeneutical lens for reading Scripture, rather than an independent authority."[256] The experience of Spirit-filled Gentiles led the church to re-examine their scriptures, and find there that inclusion of the Gentiles was God's clear intention from the covenant with Abraham on. They realised that they had misinterpreted Scripture, not that experience 'trumped' Scripture. In contrast, there are no scriptural texts which affirm God's design for human sexuality to include homosexual acts. Andrew Goddard puts it well: "It is one thing to say that, in the light of listening to and learning from the experience of other Christians,

---

252. Kathryn Greene-McCreight, "The Logic of the Interpretation of Scripture and the Church's Debate over Sexual Ethics," in *Homosexuality, Science and the "Plain Sense of Scripture,"* ed. David Balch (Grand Rapids: Eerdmans, 2000), 242-260.

253. Luke Timothy Johnson, "Debate & Discernment: Scripture & the Spirit."

254. Hays, *The Moral Vision of the New Testament*, 399.

255. Hays, *The Moral Vision of the New Testament*, 399.

256. Hays, *The Moral Vision of the New Testament*, 399.

we must go back and study the Bible afresh. It is quite another to say that listening to experience could lead a faithful Christian to the conclusion that the Bible is wrong and an unreliable guide to God's will for us."[257]

In terms of the Wesleyan/Anglican quadrilateral of Scripture, Tradition, Reason and Experience as sources of ethical authority, whether the appeal is to new knowledge or a new revelation, Scripture is no longer seen as the primary authority, but as only one source among others, which may be "trumped" by Reason or Experience. But while Reason and Experience may legitimately prompt us to reconsider our interpretation of various texts, those with a high view of Scripture will not be persuaded by arguments which seek to override its authority with any other authority.

A Study of 1 Timothy 1:8-11

Authorship

Despite the wide consensus among critical scholars that this letter, together with 2 Timothy and Titus, was written pseudonymously by a later church leader writing in the tradition of Paul, I incline to the minority, traditional interpretation that this letter was indeed written by the apostle Paul.[258] Therefore I will refer to the writer as Paul. But this presupposition is not essential to the 'conservative' argument on homosexuality. As Jenks acknowledges, "whether or not the words were written by Paul ... they remain part of the canonical Scriptures. The spiritual authority of the text derives from their canonical status within the religious community that holds them sacred."[259] And if the letter was not written by Paul, the use of the term *arsenokoitas*, coined by Paul in 1 Corinthians 6:9 and found nowhere else in the

---

257. Andrew Goddard, "The Listening Process: Listening to Learn, Learning to Listen," *Fulcrum* (2006) http://www.fulcrum-anglican.org.uk/news/2006/newsletter10.cfm?doc=149.

258. Philip H. Towner, *The Letters to Timothy and Titus* (NICNT; Grand Rapids, Michigan: Eerdmans, 2006), 10-26.

259. Jenks, "Rules for Holy Living", 73.

New Testament, and its inclusion in a similar vice list to the one in that passage, confirms that Paul's negative attitude to homosexual practice continued in the early post-Pauline churches.[260]

Context

This passage is found in the first major section of the letter written to Timothy, a young co-worker of Paul. Timothy was now a leader in the church at Ephesus, a prominent, wealthy, and religiously diverse Greek city. The church, which included both Jews and Gentiles, had been established by Paul during a brief visit (Acts 18:18-21). He later returned (Acts 19:1) and was based there for about three years.

Structure of the Argument

After the greeting, the first section of the letter (1 Tim 1:3-20) deals with false teachers and false doctrine and may be divided into four subsections: the charge to Timothy to engage with and correct these false teachers who desire to be teachers of the law "without understanding either what they are saying or the things about which they make assertions" (1:3-7); the passage before us, a discussion of the relationship between the law and Paul's gospel (1:8-11); a recounting of Paul's calling as a pattern of conversion from rebellion against God, through the mercy and grace of Christ Jesus (1:12-17); a renewal of the call to Timothy to "fight the good fight", beginning with confronting the false teachers (1:18-20).[261]

In his opening charge to Timothy, Paul reiterates a common theme in his letters, that the heart of discipleship is "love that comes from a pure heart, a good conscience and sincere faith" (1:5). He contrasts this with the message of the false teachers who want to teach the law. But in case he is misunderstood as dismissing the law altogether he affirms its usefulness: "Now we know that the law is good", echoing Romans 7:7-25 where he describes the law as 'holy' and spiritual'. The law is not a central topic in this letter, Paul has discussed it elsewhere, and we know that salvation is not a matter

---

260. Gagnon. *The Bible and Homosexual Practice,* 332.

261. Towner, *The Letters to Timothy and Titus,* 70.

of obedience to the law. The law does, however (as in Romans 7), have an ongoing function of moral instruction, for the lawless and disobedient. To illustrate this, Paul employs the rhetorical device of a vice list, but instead of the usual vices (character traits) themselves, he lists people known for certain attributes and behaviours. Thus he "creates a portrait of godless human activity that is precisely the opposite of the image of Christian activity characterised in 1:5 by love."[262] This is why Paul says that the law is not for the innocent — the godly do not need the law to know that these behaviours are wrong.

Exegetical issues

Included in the list are *pornoi* and *arsenokoitai*, "the sexually immoral," and "those practicing homosexuality." These terms have had various translations, and "sodomites" is indeed a poor translation of *arsenokoitai* (NRSV).[263] *Pornoi* is a general term referring to the sexually immoral, while *arsenokoitai* is more specific in designating something pertaining to homosexuality. Scroggs thinks *pornoi* means male prostitutes and *arsenokoitai* denotes men who have sex with male prostitutes, while Keith Dyer supposes that it "carries the added connotation of male prostitution and the economic exploitation of sex rather than 'homosexuality' as such,"[264] and Alan Cadwallader proposes that it is "someone who acts dishonourably and violently in a sexual intrusion upon the body of another."[265] These views do not have broad support

---

262. Towner, *The Letters to Timothy and Titus* 124.

263. Despite subsequent use of term 'sodomite', what the men of the city of Sodom had in mind (Gen 19) was homosexual gang rape, not consensual homosexual acts. The prophet Ezekiel explains the reason for the judgment on Sodom in terms of pride, greed and refusal to help the poor and needy (Ezek 16:49-50). Although Jude 7 refers to Sodom (and Gomorrah) indulging in sexual immorality and going after other flesh, most commentators think the latter phrase refers to the fact that Lot's visitors were angels.

264. Keith Dyer, "A Consistent Biblical Approach to '(Homo)sexuality'," in *Whose Homosexuality? Which Authority?* eds. Brian Edgar and Gordon Preece (Adelaide: ATF Press, 2006), 1-21, 18.

265. Alan Cadwallader, "Keeping Lists or Embracing Freedom," in *Five Uneasy Pieces* (Adelaide, ATF Press, 2011), 47-67, 60.

among biblical scholars, and Jenks accepts the "conservative" view that the term refers generally to "sexual activities by men with male partners."[266]

However—and this is critical to his argument—Jenks claims that the list in which *arsenokoitai* occurs is not a list of immoral behaviours, but only those behaviours which are socially inappropriate or offensive. It is, according to Jenks, "a catalogue of people whose actions make them unacceptable within polite society" and "not an explicitly religious or theological catalogue of sinful actions. Rather it is a generic list of socially unacceptable behaviours."[267] Jenks does not claim merely that this is how we should interpret these actions today (a matter of hermeneutics), but that this is what the author meant (a matter of exegesis). He gives no evidence and offers no argument in support of this claim. Yet it is simply not plausible, given that Paul describes the people who do such things as "lawless and disobedient," "godless and sinful," "unholy and profane" (v. 9), and their actions as "contrary to the sound teaching that conforms to the glorious gospel of the blessed God, which he entrusted to me" (v. 10).

If Jenks' claim is correct, it must be true of all the behaviours in the list. Did Paul (and are we to) think that murder is just a matter of being unacceptable in polite society? Or that slave trading, lying and perjury are merely socially unacceptable? Jenks realises that this is a problem for his reading of the text, and he acknowledges that "indiscriminate and promiscuous sexual activity—no matter what genders are involved—is clearly unacceptable."[268] Presumably he would say the same of all the other items in the list, except male homosexual acts. But on what basis? Jenks says that he subscribes to the spiritual authority of biblical texts,[269] but seems to be using an

---

266. Jenks, "Rules for Holy Living," 71.

267. Jenks, "Rules for Holy Living," 71.

268. Jenks, "Rules for Holy Living," 81.

269. Jenks, "Rules for Holy Living," 73.

independent moral authority other than Scripture by which to pick and choose which biblical moral teaching he accepts, though he does not explain what this other authority is.

It seems that Jenks comes to the text with a presupposition, derived from this other moral authority, that homosexual acts need not be immoral, and so attempts to twist the meaning of the text to fit with this presupposition. Exploring the meaning of *arsenokoitais* would seem a more potentially fruitful strategy for revisionists than this approach, if they wish to persuade those who read this text "conservatively" to change their mind about what it meant then, and what it means now.

In counter-point, if we adopt a canonical reading of Scripture, rather than treating this text in isolation, we can understand why Paul regards male homosexual acts as immoral. This is how Paul evidently interprets the prohibitions of Leviticus 18:22 and 20:13, based in turn on the foundational understanding of human sexuality in Genesis 1 and 2, that male and female are differentiated and complementary. This is the creation pattern for sexual relationships: "Therefore a man leaves his father and his mother and clings to his wife, and they become one flesh" (Gen 2:24). This creation design is also re-affirmed by Jesus (Mt 19:6) and by Paul in Romans 1:18-32. But Jenks tells us that his theology is "consciously progressive,"[270] where one of the defining characteristics of progressive Christianity is "transgressing gender boundaries."[271] He comes to the text with a presupposition that is in conflict with the creation story of gender differentiation and gender complementarity, and so it is not surprising that he declines to use creational categories and their corollaries as the basis of the categorisation of male homosexual acts as immoral in 1 Timothy 1:8-11.

---

270. Jenks, "Rules for Holy Living," 77.

271. Hal Tussag, *A New Spiritual Home: Progressive Christianity at the Grassroots* (Santa Rosa, CA: Polebridge, 2006), cited in Jenks, "Rules for Holy Living," 77, n.10.

Hermeneutical Issues

Jenks makes his claim about the meaning of the text because it is a necessary first step in the two step process of his argument. If homosexual practice is not a moral issue, but only one of social conventions, then Jenks' observations about the differences in cultural norms and values between the world of the biblical text and our modern Western societies becomes relevant to our interpretation of this text.[272] We can then treat Paul's teaching here as we do his instructions about head coverings, the length of hair for men, and wearing pearls or braided hair for women. That is, reinterpret them to be appropriate applications of the abiding moral principle underlying these instructions, in the context of our changed social conventions.

Jenks also appeals to a difference in understanding of sexuality between the world of the New Testament and ours. He writes: "our understanding of what it means to be human has changed radically. We have a very different view of gender and human sexuality."[273] The implication is that we not only have a different, but a better, more informed understanding of human sexuality than the primitive understanding of those in the ancient world. In her "Uneasy Piece," Peta Sherlock also appeals to this supposed evolution in our understanding. She argues that what Paul condemns in Romans 1 is homosexual behaviour motivated by greed and lust, rather than homosexual acts in a committed and faithful relationship, because "he seems to have no understanding of people who are genuinely 'naturally' homosexual."[274] She cites Walter Wink s claim that Paul had no concept of homosexual orientation. According to Wink, Paul thought everyone was straight, no one is homosexual by nature, and so all homosexual behaviour must be "unnatural." [275]

---

272. Jenks, "Rules for Holy Living," 72.

273. Jenks, "Rules for Holy Living," 80.

274. Peta Sherlock, "Reading Romans as Anglicans- Romans 1:26-27," in *Five Uneasy Pieces* 31-45, 41.

275. Wink, "Homosexuality and the Bible," www.soulforce.org/article/

But was Paul really unaware of what we now call a homosexual orientation? It was well known in ancient Greek culture, as was the idea that homosexuals are born and not made, as the creation myth in Plato's symposium attests.[276] Revisionist scholars are increasingly acknowledging that Paul could well have known that some people had a lifelong pattern of homosexual relationships, some of which were loving and committed. Gay sociologist Stephen Murray says, "I consider it incredibly arrogant—specifically chronocentric and ethnocentric—to proclaim that no one recognised homosexual desires before the late nineteenth century forensic psychiatrists wrote about it ... Many languages have labels for kinds of persons known to engage in it recurrently."[277] Bernadette Brooten concludes from her study of homosexuality and lesbianism in particular in the ancient world, that, "Paul could have believed that *tribades* (lesbians), *kinaidoi* (effeminate) and other sexually unorthodox persons were born that way and yet still condemn them as unnatural and shameful."[278]

It is sometimes asserted that the only form of homosexual activity Paul would have known about was exploitative, between older males and young men or slaves. An aggressive and exploitive bisexuality was most probably dominant, but it was certainly not the only kind of homosexual relationship known in antiquity. As Gagnon comments: "Moving statements about the compassionate and beautiful character of same-sex love can be found in Graeco-

---

homosexuality-bible-walter-wink.

276. This contains a story of humans created as "doubles," with two heads, four arms, and four legs. Some were male/female combinations, some male/male and some female/female. According to this myth, they were then split in half by the gods, leaving each half with a desperate longing for the separated one (Robert Williams, "Toward a Theology for Lesbian and Gay Marriage" in *Christian Perspectives on Sexuality and Gender* eds. Adrian Thatcher and Elizabeth Stuart [Grand Rapids: Eerdmans, 1996], 79-300).

277. Stephen O. Murray, *Homosexualities* (Chicago: University of Chicago Press, 2000), 8.

278. Bernadette Brooten, *Love Between Women* (Chicago and London: University of Chicago Press, 1996), 233.

Roman literature."[279] Mark Smith describes examples which refer not only to love between men and boys or youths, but between males of roughly equal age, and between females, with many of these characterised as stable, even lifelong, and concludes that Paul "probably did know of at least several types of homosexual practices among both men and women."[280]

Conclusion

If Jenks' reading of the text is simply not plausible, no amount of discussion about the hermeneutical dance or reader-response theory[281] will allow an interpretation that flatly contradicts the original meaning of the text.

Jenks' argument amounts to this, that the writer of 1 Timothy undoubtedly found homosexual acts unacceptable, but "[w]hat our ancestors found offensive may not offend us."[282] In the end, the question of the morality of homosexual acts comes down to what the reader does or does not find offensive. In other words, morality has been reduced to aesthetics. Such a subjective approach is likely to be as unsatisfactory to revisionists as to conservatives. It provides no objective grounds upon which to critique either view. If one can say, "What you find offensive, I do not," then the other can equally validly retort, "And what you do not find offensive, I do." But revisionists and conservatives are both convinced that the church ought to adopt one view and policy on the matter. Either accept that faithful homosexual relationships are compatible with Christian discipleship, or that they are not. Either ordain practising gay and lesbians, and bless homosexual unions, or do not. For revisionists,

---

279.   Gagnon, *The Bible and Homosexual Practice*, 350-358. Gagnon cites extensively from Plato's *Symposium,* and the *Pseudo-Lucianic Affairs of the Heart.*

280.   Mark D. Smith, "Ancient Bisexuality and the Interpretation of Romans 1:26-27," *Journal of the American Academy of Religion* 64 (1996): 223-56, 247.

281.   For a critique of reader-response theory, see Kevin J. Vanhoozer, *Is There a Meaning in this Text?* (Grand Rapids, Michigan: Zondervan, 1998).

282.   Jenks, "Rules for Holy Living," 80-81.

"[t]his is not just an issue concerning private morality ... It is a justice issue- an issue of righteousness in the private and public spheres— and a matter of life and death for some in our community."[283] For conservatives, this is also an issue of righteousness: submission to the authority of God in Scripture and living a godly life is fundamental to Christian discipleship. Both revisionists and conservatives think this is too important an issue to be simply a matter of personal feelings. Conservatives are convinced, however, that their view is the one which is more faithful to Scripture, rightly interpreted.

---

283. Dyer, "A Consistent Biblical Approach to '(Homo)sexuality,'" 4-5.

CHAPTER 7
Listening to a Complex Story

BARRY MCGRATH

We all want to be accepted. It is one of our primary drives as people. We want people to accept us into their community and understand who we are. We long and hope for the embrace of others who will take us into their hearts. At best, churches are places where people find a home; where people find a community which embraces them. The embrace is not as the culture around us, for with Christ's people there should be no weighing of ability and skill; no gauging of worth of value by career, or position or wealth; there is the acceptance that we are Christ's and we are called into community.

One of the challenges in discussing areas of sexual ethics is the very real issue of how we deal with this at the local church level. How do we deal with members of our churches when they are honestly struggling with these issues in their study of the scriptures? How do we deal with those who are struggling with same-sex attraction? How do we deal with those who see no conflict between their homosexual behaviour and their Christian faith?

The head in the sand approach is just never going to work. We can avoid talking about sexuality; we can just presume that everyone has no issues around sexuality, but that approach lacks authenticity. Denial also deprives people of a voice. Many in our communities will have issues and questions and alternative views and it is beholden on the leadership of a church community to create an atmosphere where people are not fearful to consider the uncomfortable, the different, and the areas of our life which challenge and provoke.

Acceptance does not mean that we can or will agree. To always agree would be impossible. Yet we need to search for a model of being in our church communities where we can open the conversation about sexuality under the Word of God. To stand with our brothers and sisters in Christ and consider together what the scriptures are saying, not what our culture is saying about sexuality.

Acceptance will be found in honestly engaging with the scriptures and moving forward as a community. Too often churches do not openly deal with the sexual ethics in the scriptures, as it can offend and challenge and create dissension. This leaves those with particular issues on the outside. Shouldn't we bring into the open the mess and complexity of our lives? In that open space before God let us accept each other and be open to consider change and repentance and forgiveness and new ways of being.

If we are open to the voice of God in our church communities we will be able to come together as one. Under Christ we have been given an extraordinary opportunity to be new creations. We have been given the opportunity to be members of Christ's body. In that community of saints we can find acceptance, all together under Christ.

Yet the call on us as a holy and obedient community is not to be accepting of sin, nor lifestyles which move us away from Christ rather than towards a godly life. To consider sexual ethics in the Bible we will name sin and we will be called to repent. And at times we will break fellowship as our goal is never mere acceptance, it is the holy life.

Engaging in the critical conversation

The pastor is the listener.

The pastor listens to the Word of God and to their flock. They listen to the hubbub of the culture around them, seeking out the zeitgeist from the cultural dialogue. They listen to people's stories of their struggles and their joys; their wrestling with issues and contradictions. They listen to God's Word in all its fullness and richness.

The pastor is the listener. They listen for nuance and the cadence of a story. They listen for the heart of the story and the real issues, even if they are not obvious on first hearing. They listen to the scriptures, with scholarship and heart, to see how this revelation can be spoken into lives.

For the pastor is the speaker as well. The listening leads into engagement and application. And in this speaking is the delicate and bold task of seeing how God's Word can be spoken and heard. There is the prophetic task of the pastor to hear God's Word as the pre-eminent story and to speak it into the lives of the saints.

When hearing stories of identity and sexuality it is beholden on the pastor to listen with sensitivity and with insight. To hear a person's story, and to have empathy, or least a glimmer of comprehension of what has gone on for the other, is crucial if the pastor is to importantly take the person with them to uncover the voice of God in their circumstance. For that surely is where the pastor, as shepherd of the flock, needs to guide the conversation. God must have the clearest voice in all the vicissitudes of our life, and especially in pastoral work, otherwise the pastor denudes the ministry of its heart, and starves the saint, who has come to them, of the spiritual food of the scriptures, where we find succour and nourishment.

As a pastor of 20 years I have found the task of listening a privilege. To hear another's story is to have opened for us the depth of our humanity. To be a pastor is to hear the complexity of the human condition. People rarely come to their minister just to meet with them and tell them how great their life is going. The saints come with their dilemmas and their woes; they come with troubled relationships and with shame and embarrassment; they come wrestling with how to live out the teaching of Jesus.

The temptation as a pastor is to listen and agree with what the other says. We all want to be liked. The pastor is no exception. One does not lose their humanity when pastoring, nor their own desires for acceptance. Yet the pastor is not to seek affirmation nor acceptance, rather their role is to hear, and consider, and lead the saints to Christ, and offer a way forward.

Our faith in Christ is resurrection faith. The power of a faith which is stronger than death is what we take into any pastoral conversation. Illness is never the end of the story, nor despair, nor death, nor sexuality. We have been shown the vista of a life of meaning and hope with our faith in the risen Lord Jesus. No matter how overwhelming the circumstances, the saints have clung tenaciously, especially in suffering, to a holy and obedient life in Christ.

The pastor is the listener. And over the years I have heard so many stories of people's issues and struggles with the expression of their sexuality. The challenge is always to lead them to Christ. The challenge is to allow the voice of Scripture to speak. Pastors are not here to merely affirm desires, they have the task of facilitating a hearing for God's Word.

The hearing of God's Word in our sexuality and relationships is one of the grand challenges we have as 21st century people. It is so counter cultural to consider that our desires do not forge our meaning. It is profoundly countercultural to open ourselves to God's Word and hear what it has to say, when we just don't want to hear. It is a challenge to consider that God's voice may be authoritative in our loves and affections and desires.

Whose advice do we heed? What are the signposts that we pay attention to? In our culture the story of the self can be the loudest story. It can hail down the voice of God. "This is now I feel" and "This is my experience" can become the untouchable truths that we must heed. Yet the pastor's task is to primarily always hear the voice of God and to assist others in their hearing.

The voice of God in the Scriptures is the voice of the Father God calling his children; it is the voice of the father of the prodigal as he runs to embrace his lost son. It is a voice which is both authoritative and comforting; a voice which encourages and admonishes; a voice which judges and offers hope. It is the voice we are called to listen to as God's people. As author of Hebrews admonishes us: "See to it that you do not refuse him who speaks" (Heb 12:25).

And as saints we wrestle with that voice in our lives. In the midst of relational difficulty it is so pleasant to hear the words of sympathy and empathy, yet the saints want something more. We want to hear the voice of God challenging, admonishing and encouraging. In the midst of relational difficulty who wants to be encouraged to submit to one another out of reverence for Christ? We can nod meaningfully at the words but in our hearts we can be struggling. God has spoken through His prophets and finally through His Son, and the saints are hard of hearing.

My encouragement in pastoral ministry is that we have the voice of the scriptures to guide us and assist us to negotiate the way ahead. And in the area of relationships and sexuality, it is comforting to have a fast anchor for our ministry. The voice of our culture is loud and intrusive and can be abrasive to those seeking to hear God in the mire that is us seeking identity and meaning. In the area of sexual identity our culture has been unhelpful for so many, as it has sought to simplify sexuality and identity, rather than cope with the complexity of human sexuality.

Simplifying Sexuality

The twenty something man who comes to see me about his sexuality does not fit easily into categories of gay and straight. He is a celibate young man who is in love with a young woman from his church. They have been dating for a year and the relationship looks to both of them like it has a future. They have spoken of marriage and in the midst of this relationship he comes to talk to me.

This young man is sexually attracted to his girlfriend and recognises that he is also same-sex attracted. The simple approach may be to tell him he really is gay and that he needs to face up to that reality. Conversely, he could be told that he is straight and he needs to just disregard these other desires. Yet the labels, gay or straight, come nowhere near approximating the complexity of his sexuality and his hopes and desires for the future, and his desire to lead a godly and obedient life.

The woman who ends up in bed with a female friend could be read simply as a woman who has finally discovered her true identity. Yet for her it was a surprising and regretful event. She did not want to have sex outside the confines of a marriage between a man and a woman.

The man who has had numerous sexual partners on beats and in clubs in Sydney, who comes to church, owns the title Christian. He feels caught in an addictive cycle with his sexual attraction to men. He is straightforward in his acknowledgement that how he is living does not fit into his faith. He is not naïve. And he does not own the title "gay". He knows his behaviour is clearly homosexual, yet his primary identity is not his sexual expression, rather it is his relationship with Christ.

If these three stories were reported in the press I would be surprised if the nuance would be reported. I would be surprised if the journalists could report without resorting to labels. The labels make shallow these people's identity. They don't see themselves as gay, they see themselves as Christians who are working through living a godly life. They don't want to embrace a lifestyle where a label is attached to them, which declares their sexuality as their primary nomenclature.

But in our culture we can't seem to deal with complexity. Has the church drunk of this simplification of identity? Do we define people according to their sexual behaviour as if that says something of them beyond what they do with their bodies? Do we define people according to their desires, even if they don't act upon them?

It is ironic that so many people have felt the cruel weight of labels in their school years and then embrace them in their adult years. So many people with same-sex desires have been taunted as teenagers, with labels trying to sum up their whole identity, and then cling tenaciously to the same labels in adulthood. Identification with a label can provide a level of security and belonging, yet it can be a misplaced confidence. The impact of a faith in Christ is surely that we have a new identity of being found in Him. To be "in Christ" is the primary identity of the believer, so it seems to be contrary to that grand ascription to want to define our humanity by our sexual behaviour and sexual attraction.

Our identity is that we are saints. As soon as we have another title or identity that overwhelms the description of us as saints it is a denigration of the holiness that has been given us by the grace of God. We live in a culture which wants to define us by sexuality—Gay/Lesbian/Straight/Bi/Transgender. The straightjacket of defining our humanity by behaviour is an oddly truncated view of humanity. We are made in the image of God, and so have intrinsic dignity and worth. To be defined by a passing desire is a barely polite nod to the fullness of life Jesus offers us in John 10:10.

Over my ministry years I have found it unhelpful to classify people according to their sexuality. The labels never seem to be full enough to encompass someone's history, experience, feelings or behaviour. A label of gay or straight is a *cul-de-sac* pastorally—a dead end where we reach an impasse which says that my sexual identity is immoveable. Pastorally, if people cling tenaciously to any identity outside of "in Christ" then they set up a barrier to hearing the voice of God speaking into their life.

The language of lobby groups and politicians is a language which simplifies. The lobby group has the language of the goodies and the baddies; the language of those in and those out. It may have served lobby groups working for the position of some to push that we are divided into sexual groupings, yet is it a way forward for the church? Is our sexuality far more complex than us being placed in clear groupings?

When the actor Cynthia Nixon stated that she had chosen to be a lesbian, there was a level of outrage among many in the lesbian community. The idea that one could be exclusively heterosexual and then choose to be exclusively homosexual is an offence to the simple categories of gay and straight. No wonder her situation raised the ire of so many. For in her story we have the notion of choice; we have the flexibility of labels; and we have an individual who refuses a simple category.

The anxiety in Cynthia Nixon's description of her sexuality is that if sexuality could be a choice then it questions the notion that people are born with a particular sexuality and orientation. It is a lobby group battle, rather than listening to the reality that for many people their sexuality does involve choice and decision. For many people that I have encountered in pastoral ministry, there are choices to be made about desires which arise in our life. It may be unpalatable to those who consider that our sexuality is imprinted and undeniable, that there is choice in our sexual expression, yet it may be an uncomfortable truth we need to consider in our churches.

Choices on how to respond to our desires, even our sexual desires, are made constantly by us all. A desire arises and we act, but in that space between the arising and the action is a complex web of decisions. And to have a desire is not the same as the assumption of a sexual identity. A sexual identity arises from a complex web of history, desire, and the culture where we live and the relationships in which we engage.

The Cynthia Nixon press coverage reported the political implications of choice. There were commentators who were angered about what she had said as they saw it having implications for how the GLBT community is seen. It highlighted that the issue of sexuality is politicised and it is difficult to hear complexity and nuance.

The middle-aged man who has felt sexual attraction to men since his teenage years can easily be classified as gay in the conversation of our culture. When we find out that he has been celibate all his life due to his Christian faith we can read him as an oppressed individual who has had his real identity denied him by a repressive church. And then when he fell in love with a woman at his church and married and ended up in a sexually satisfying relationship with his wife, what category do we put him in then? Has he denied his true self or has he found it? Is he just fooling himself and his wife or has he recognised that some of his desires do not predicate his life or his faith?

My experience in the pastorate has shown me that sexual identity labels don't mean much. They speak of a shallow description of one part of a person's life, but they are never the full picture. Labels can be useful in the static environment of the museum, but in the dynamic life of the Christian there is so much more to this life than our sexual desires and behaviours.

One of the problems of the simple labels of GLBT is that they can destructively make some Christians feel that they are stuck. To have a particular desire is no big deal really, but if you are then labelled with an identity for that desire then your freedom is curtailed. For the Christian believer to be told that a desire that they experience is actually their immovable identity is to imprison many in a straightjacket of labelling.

The believer who has primarily engaged in sex with those of their own gender is not necessarily the person who wants to wear the label gay or lesbian. For many believers it is an issue of not wanting to be labelled by their sin. The easy way out could be to say that having sex with those of your own gender is just not sin. Yet for many Christians they cannot make that jump as their understanding of biblical sexuality does not allow them that license.

The experiential truth of so many Christians is that their sexual desires do not make them. Same-sex attraction is for many not a core identity, it is merely a part of their sexuality. It has been destructive to have a lobby group attempting to deny people their freedom to live obedient lives to their biblical faith.

The hermeneutical jumps that are made by some in the church in their attempt to justify homosexual acts are a planet away from many people in churches. Many Christians read the scriptures and are given the clear impression that a godly expression of sexuality only resides within marriage of a man and a woman or chastity. They see the normative path of sexuality in the scriptures and want to follow that path in their desire to live holy and obedient lives. It is not just five short sections in the Bible that Christians read and hear a message about homosexuality, it is that full and clear message which believers read and hear, that fulfilling sexual expression is found in the oneness spoken of by Jesus, between man and woman.

It is a neat label to somehow bundle up someone's identity with a tag like gay or bi or straight. It is the language of a consumerist culture, where we all fit into neat categories where we can be marketed. Yet the saints have a far richer identity that we regularly need to remind each other of, that we are Christ's and our desires are not the source of our identity.

Sex in a consumerist culture

One of the challenges the church faces in our culture is our attachment to personal desire as a virtue. The heart of consumerist society is founded on our desires as the prime movers for our action. We want a product for the satisfaction it brings, so we purchase. Consumerism is the prop to our personal desires, it is our *raison d'etre*.

We live in a society where the ubiquitous language and imagery of advertising sells a vision of our humanity which is a long way from the dignity and significance we see in the Bible. The language of the advertiser is the language of desire.

Advertising addresses us as beings of desire who can be satisfied with the purchase of a product or service. We are addressed as those who can purchase satisfaction. Our desires will be met. It is normal now for so many products to be advertised as a bespoke answer to our desires. Of course it is a lie, but it is so appealing to have every whim and fancy satisfied with a credit card.

I do wonder what a consumerist culture has done to our faith? What is the impact of living in a culture where the traditional virtue of patience is seen as an irrelevance? Why not get satisfaction now? What is the impact on our chastity when we are told that we should live out our sexual desires without limit?

To be true to yourself has been translated into doing what you feel. So it seems a denial of our humanity to choose to reject what we desire or how we feel. We stand up for people's desires in our culture. If you want something then that is a good. To discover what you want is to somehow uncover a true self. Yet what if our desires are not our primary motivators, but something larger, something more virtuous, something godly? We live in a time when it just seems right to follow your dreams; to express exactly what is in your heart and mind; to sexually express yourself. And the only proviso is "as long as you don't hurt anyone, all is well."

Yet, this is a long way from the biblical idea of contentment. Proverbs warn us of our desires which can so easily lead us astray (Pr 12:12, 13:4, 21:10). The Psalmist (Ps 51) bemoans our entrenched sinfulness from birth, and St Paul notes the desires of the flesh which war against the life of the Spirit (Rom 7, Gal 5). In our culture it is hard to hear that our natural desires may not be the measure of the virtuous life. It can be difficult to see that what we feel may not be what should be expressed; or that what we want sexually does not indicate how God sees our sexuality.

In pastoral ministry it is of course good for people to uncover their desires. It is good to be honest and to have a recognition of what we feel. And it is appropriate that we take the next step to consider what desires are appropriate for God's person to act upon. This is so crucial in terms of our sexuality. The deep challenge in our cultural context is that we may need to name some of our desires as sin.

The role of the pastor and the church is not to condemn those who have desires at odds with their faith, rather the church is to be a haven of acceptance. We are all broken individuals who need Christ. We are called to be supportive fellowships which assist each other to love the Lord and love each other. Our call is to journey with each other through change as we are conformed into the likeness of Christ.

The common celibate

Churches are full of people who lead celibate lives. In such a sexualised culture it seems anathema to say that some live without having sex, yet for so many Christians that is the reality of their lives. Many people just do not find a marriage partner. Many people read the scriptures and consider that only in marriage can they have a sexual relationship, and as they are not married, celibacy is the godly option.

Celibacy is the option for the grand majority of believers at some time in their lives. We do not live in a culture where we get married as soon as we reach puberty. Young people in a myriad of church communities are encouraged to live celibate lives until they find a life partner. Most of us will be celibate at several points in our life— that is normal.

And for those of us who have chosen marriage, it is a deaf pastor who has not heard of the many couples who cannot have a sexual life at some period in their marriage. The person who cares long term for their ill husband or wife and cannot have a sexual relationship is not that unusual. So many couples face celibacy in their marriages due to mental health and other serious health issues.

And then there are those whose husbands or wives die and leave them alone; those who are betrayed and their spouses leave them for someone else; those who are unable to have sex due to a medical condition; those who are forced by circumstances beyond their control to live apart. A few years ago was speaking at a theological college in Africa and met so many pastors who had to leave their wives for years due to the pressures of poverty and oppression, and so chose to live celibate lives

So celibacy is not unusual in our churches. Nor has it ever been. Christians who want to live holy and obedient lives often choose to not have sex. There are those who have taken seriously the injunction to not marry an unbeliever and so have chosen a life of celibacy. There are those who have taken their marriage vows seriously and so have had to live a celibate life as their partner is unable to engage with them sexually. There are those people who are just not that sexual and they would prefer not to have sex with others. And I could go on with the many reasons why Christians choose celibacy.

Celibacy is not a disaster. It is not a failure. It does not mean that we are worthless. It does not indicate anything about self worth. Jesus was celibate. St Paul sees it as liberation from marital duties (1 Cor 7:8-9, 25-31). Celibacy is not an aberration but a choice many wise and godly Christians have made over the centuries.

The celibate Christians in our church communities do not make a lobby group. One cannot define them by their sexuality. One cannot lump them altogether. They are merely a large group of people that many of us most probably will join at different times in our life.

The option for the same-sex attracted person is in many cases celibacy. Imagine encouraging people to lead a celibate life! It is such a countercultural statement. Yet it is what we do in responsible pastoring all the time with a wide range of people, not just those who are same-sex attracted. For so many people the option if they are not to be sexually immoral, is to be celibate.

The encouragement to be chaste sounds quaint at best. In our culture it seems oppressive and foreign to the sexual liberty which we espouse. Imagine encouraging someone to not act on their sexuality? Imagine encouraging someone to be celibate? It really is foreign to the sexual mores of so many in the 21st century. But the Christian path is rarely mainstream. The pastor's role is not to encourage their flock to live in a way which is normative in a particular society, rather we are to "shine as lights in the world" (Phil 1:15).

Celibacy is a hard road for some, and others find it a passing challenge, whereas some find it relatively easy. Those who find it difficult are those who the pastor so often encounters. The challenges and difficulties of a life do not alter the truth of God's people leading holy sexual lives. The pastors and fellowship of any church need to support and encourage those who have chosen the path of obedience.

To encourage anyone to live a celibate life means one must lead them to the scriptures so that they can hear the voice of God themselves. The individual needs to do business with God rather than with their minister. It is not an enforcing of a lifestyle upon people, rather it is assisting a person as they make decisions which may be hard to live out. The church is called to support, encourage, love and nurture those who make this decision to live in a way "worthy of the gospel" (Phil 1:27).

And what of those who make a decision but fail in its execution? Those folk join the endless line of all those who know they need the Lord Jesus. We not only have a Lord but we have a Saviour who is the harbinger and deliverer of forgiveness into our messy and broken lives. Our failure to live the lives we want to live does not mean though that we just change our standards. It means that we recognise at every point our need for Christ; our dependence upon Him; and His limitless love for us.

The reality of change

One of the most challenging aspects of the discussion about sexuality in our cultural context is listening to people's stories of change. There are many people who have had an identity which is GLBT and are now living radically different lives.

The stories of these people are stories of transformation. In my discussions with some of them it is not about healing but about change after a decision to follow Christ. People do live in the gay and lesbian communities and are sexually active and then change. It does not fit the rhetoric of those who say that we are what we are, but it is a reality within our churches.

If our sexuality is completely set and there is no escape from that orientation it is a very neat story. The simple story that you are born gay is an easy story, yet so many people have a different story to tell. People in and out of the church have made decisions about their sexuality, to act not on same-sex desire. For some that has led them to heterosexual relationships, and for others it has led them to a life of celibacy.

There are alternative stories around sexuality which we can listen to, not just the standard story that our sexual preference is set. Many people have decided to not live out a particular set of desires around their sexuality. It may not be a palatable story to some, yet it is a story which cannot be silenced.

A woman I know turned to Christ at 16. Her same-sex attraction was a battle and struggle. She felt isolated and lonely in her predicament. Sadly, she could not talk to anyone about how she felt about her sexuality. At 21 she decided to go to a church which embraced her lesbian attraction and encouraged her to embrace her sexuality.

The three years she was a part of that church was a time of exploration for her, yet it did not eventuate in the liberty she hoped for. She may have found a church which affirmed her sexuality yet ... she could not agree with their teaching on sexuality as it was at a remove from what she read in God's Word. Try as she might to protect her lesbian identity she was torn between a desire to be true to the faith she had uncovered in the scriptures and her integrity as a person.

She ended up leaving the church which told her it was fine for her to be lesbian and made a decision to go to a church which embraced a traditional biblical position on sexuality. She chose to live a life where she would not pursue her desire for other women. Talking to her is not a tale of repression, it is the story of someone making a decision about how she wants to live as God's person. Life is rarely straightforward and easy, but people like this woman have found a peace in leading a life of obedience. She is not looking to be heterosexual, nor to be cured; she is merely seeking to live a holy and obedient life. We may not choose our desires, but neither do our desires have to make our choices for us.

This woman's story could have been very different if the church had been willing in her teenage years to hear her story. She really was forced away from her church by its resistance to hearing her struggles around her sexuality. Why was there not an openness to listening to the story of her sexuality? Churches need to repent of an atmosphere where the saints cannot be open and safe with their struggles and the complexity of their sexuality.

The road ahead

There is not some place in the future where sexuality is neat, and organised. There is not some place in the future of churches where sexuality is not problematic and complex and challenging. It is mythic to consider that if we just get a bit more open and relaxed then sexuality will cease to be a fraught area in our churches.

The Bible is a story of the complexity of sexual relations. From David's misadventures to the woman at the well, the Bible records that often our sexuality is a part of the narrative of brokenness that is our life. It is buying the myths of the 60s sexual revolution to think that there is freedom to be had if we just break free of the fetters of tradition. The Bible shows us that it will always be a challenging path for the believer to negotiate this life. Sexual expression and desire melds into that mix of the complex life where we struggle to live in a way which gives honour to the life God has gifted us with, while recognising the fractured nature of so many of our desires.

Pastorally, churches will always be assisting and nurturing people in their walk with the Lord. Sexuality will always be an area where we sin so easily and so destructively. There is no easy turn in the road when all will be easy and straightforward. The great joy of sex is perhaps the great challenge, for how do we harness this desire so it is not our master but is a servant in the service of our faith?

Whatever decisions synods make; whatever pronouncements theologians make; whichever hierarchy declares a position on sexuality, as pastors we will still be left with God's people trying to work out how to live godly lives. The Bible speaks to Christians across the globe in straightforward terms about their sexuality, so pastors will continue to hear stories of people wanting change. Pastors will continue to see people repent and make choices about their sexual behaviour, driven by the desire to please their Lord.

The future for the church in terms of sexuality is that we continue to be the open communities where anyone can come and hear God speak. Churches need to be places where people can repent and turn to Christ. They need to be havens where people can be honest and find a fellowship which affirms our need of the Saviour. We are to be communities where we can name our struggles and weaknesses, without fear of the condescension of the pious. Churches are to be where love flourishes, and in our differences we still strive to love those who name Jesus as Lord and Saviour.

And pastors need to continue to listen.